FREUD AND THE LEGA

Freud's last book, *Moses and Monotheism*, was published in 1939 during one of the darkest periods in Jewish history. His scandalous and difficult book frequently has been vilified and dismissed because Freud claims that Moses was not a Hebrew but an Egyptian, and he also claims that the Jews murdered Moses in the wilderness. Bernstein argues that a close reading of *Moses and Monotheism* reveals an underlying powerful coherence in which Freud seeks to specify the distinctive character and contribution of the Jewish people. The legacy of the strict ethical monotheism of Moses is the progress of spirituality (the advance in intellectuality). It is the character that has enabled the Jewish people to survive despite persecution and virulent anti-semitism, and Freud proudly identifies himself with this legacy of Moses. In his analysis of Freud's often misunderstood last work, Bernstein goes on to show how Freud expands and deepens our understanding of a religious tradition by revealing its unconscious dynamics.

Richard J. Bernstein is Vera List Professor of Philosophy in the Graduate Faculty at the New School for Social Research, New York. His many publications include *Hannah Arendt and the Jewish Question* (Polity Press, 1996), *The New Constellation: The Ethical-Political Horizons of Modernity / Postmodernity* (Polity Press, 1991), and *Philosophical Profiles: Essays in a Pragmatic Mode* (Polity Press, 1986).

CAMBRIDGE STUDIES IN RELIGION AND CRITICAL THOUGHT

Edited by
WAYNE PROUDFOOT, *Columbia University*
JEFFREY L. STOUT, *Princeton University*
NICHOLAS WOLTERSTORFF, *Yale University*

Current events confirm the need to understand religious ideas and institutions critically, yet radical doubts have been raised about how to proceed and about the ideal of critical thought itself. Meanwhile, some prominent scholars have urged that we turn the tables, and view modern society as the object of criticism and a religious tradition as the basis for critique. Cambridge Studies in Religion and Critical Thought is a series of books intended to address the interaction of critical thinking and religious traditions in this context of uncertainty and conflicting claims. It will take up questions such as the following, either by reflecting on them philosophically or by pursuing their ramifications in studies on specific figures and movements: is a coherent critical perspective on religion desirable or even possible? What sort of relationship to religious traditions ought a critic to have? What, if anything, is worth saving from the Enlightenment legacy or from critics of religion like Hume and Feuerbach? The answers offered, while varied, will uniformly constitute distinguished, philosophically informed, and critical analyses of particular religious topics.

Titles published in the series

FREUD AND THE LEGACY OF MOSES

RICHARD J. BERNSTEIN

CAMBRIDGE
UNIVERSITY PRESS

PUBLISHED BY THE PRESS SYNDICATE OF THE UNIVERSITY OF CAMBRIDGE
The Pitt Building, Trumpington Street, Cambridge CB2 1RP, United Kingdom

CAMBRIDGE UNIVERSITY PRESS
The Edinburgh Building, Cambridge CB2 2RU, United Kingdom
40 West 20th Street, New York, NY 10011-4211, USA
10 Stamford Road, Oakleigh, Melbourne 3166, Australia

First published 1998

Printed in the United Kingdom at the University Press, Cambridge

Typeset in Baskerville 11/12.5 pt VN

A catalogue record for this book is available from the British Library

Library of Congress cataloguing in publication data
Bernstein, Richard J.
Freud and the legacy of Moses/Richard J. Bernstein.
p.   cm. – (Cambridge studies in religion and critical thought; 4)
Includes bibliographical references and index.
ISBN 0 521 63096 7 (hardback). – ISBN 0 521 63877 1 (paperback)
1. Psychoanalysis and religion.   2. Freud, Sigmund, 1856–1939 – Religion.
I. Title.   II. Series.
BF 175.7.R44B46   1998
222'.1092–dc21   98–14400   CIP

ISBN 0 521 630967 hardback
ISBN 0 521 638771 paperback

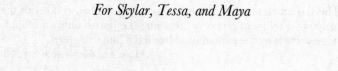

For Skylar, Tessa, and Maya

There is an element of grandeur about everything to do with the origin of a religion, certainly including the Jewish one, and that is not matched by the explanations we have hitherto given.

Moses and Monotheism (23:128)

We wanted to explain the origin of the special character of the Jewish people, a character which is probably what has made their survival to the present day possible. *Moses and Monotheism* (23:123)

Contents

Preface

Moses and Monotheism, the last book that Freud published, is one of his most difficult, perplexing, and thought-provoking works. Throughout his life Freud was deeply attracted to the figure of Moses. In his final years, he was literally obsessed with "the great man" Moses and his vexed legacy – a legacy that is rooted in the past, shapes the present, and extends its influence to the future. Freud was originally hesitant about publishing his *Moses* book, and there were those who pleaded with him to refrain from publishing it, or at least to modify some of his more shocking assertions. Writing on the eve of the Holocaust during the darkest period of Jewish history, Freud's emphatic claims that Moses was an Egyptian and that the Israelites murdered Moses in the wilderness are not only scandalous but appear to be without any solid historical foundation. Why would Freud even publish such a book? And yet, there is also a compelling grandeur about Freud's portrait of Moses and the monotheism that he professed.

When the book was first published in 1939, it provoked several polemical attacks. Even Freud's admirers were embarrassed by this awkward and confusing work. Because Freud's "arguments" were so manifestly outrageous, commentators tended to focus on the search for Freud's hidden or unconscious motives, what the book revealed about his personal conflicts, rather than on a careful analysis of what he actually says.

For many years I have returned over and over again to Freud's *Moses* study. I have long felt that the most important part of the story that Freud tells has to do with his struggle to articulate what he passionately believed to be the essence of (his) Jewishness, the key to Jewish survival, and the deep psychological reasons for anti-Semitism. The thesis that I seek to defend in this book is that Freud is attempting to answer a question that he posed for himself in the preface to the Hebrew translation of *Totem and Taboo*. Freud characterizes himself as someone who has not only abandoned the religion of his fathers, but is estranged from all religion. He then asks: "'Since you have abandoned all these common characteristics of your countrymen, what is there left to you that is Jewish?'" And he replies "'A very great deal, and probably its very essence.'" He confesses that he cannot express that essence clearly in words, but he expects that someday the answer "will become accessible to the scientific mind."[1] The answer to this question is to be found in *Moses and Monotheism* (or as I prefer to say, for reasons that I will indicate, *The Man Moses and the Monotheistic Religion* – the literal translation of the original German title of the published book).

During the first few decades after its publication, there was little serious detailed discussion of Freud's *Moses* book. But during the past decade the situation has radically changed; there has been a virtual explosion of interest in it. It is almost as if there is now a *belated* recognition that *The Man Moses and the Monotheistic Religion* is one of Freud's greatest achievements. Many thinkers, pursuing quite independent lines of inquiry, have been intrigued by the drama of Freud's narrative of the Egyptian origin of Moses and the vicissitudes of his ethically demanding monotheism in shaping the character of the Jewish people. One book in particular, Yosef Hayim Yerushalmi's *Freud's Moses: Judaism Terminable and Interminable*, has played an enormous role in raising the level of critical discussion. Yerushalmi brings his comprehensive knowledge of the Jewish tradition and his skills as a superb historian of Jewish history to bear on his analysis. Although I admire Yerushalmi's eloquence and his judicious insight, I do not think he has done full justice to Freud. Indeed, I even think that when he criticizes Freud for basing his understanding of the Jewish tradition on a "discredited Lamarckism," Yerushalmi obscures and distorts some of Freud's most creative and fertile suggestions. I have also been influenced by Jacques Derrida's *Archive Fever* – a study in which Derrida comments extensively on Yerushalmi's book. For reasons that I will set forth, I agree with many of Derrida's critical and deconstructive remarks. When I completed the initial draft of this book, I had the good fortune to read the proofs of Jan Assmann's *Moses the Egyptian: The Memory of Egypt in Western Monotheism*. Assmann is one of the world's foremost Egyptologists. Although he employs his sophisticated knowledge of Egyptian history, texts, and theology in his interpretation of Freud, his primary concern is with what he calls "mnemohistory," the history of the cultural memory of Moses as an Egyptian in Western monotheism. I have sought to take account of Assmann's strikingly original approach to Freud's *Moses* study. The fact that three such eminent thinkers from different disciplines and cultural backgrounds have been drawn to *The Man Moses and the Monotheistic Religion* is itself forceful testimony to the power of Freud's last book.

I want to clarify the interpretive stance that I have taken in this book. I am convinced that we have not yet fully come to grips with what Freud says, nor have we fully appropriated the fertility of Freud's rethinking of what a religious tradition involves, and of the unconscious dynamics of the transmission of a religious tradition. I also think that, in the final analysis, Freud does not do full justice to the meaning of Judaism and Jewishness. He tends to underestimate the creative importance of rituals, ceremonies, narratives, customs, and cultural practices that are the vehicles for (consciously and unconsciously) transmitting what *he* singles out as the great achievement of Mosaic monotheism, *Der Fortschritt in der Geistigkeit* ("The Advance in Intellectuality" or "The Progress in Spirituality"). I have refrained from developing these criticisms here because I believe that informed critique can be based only on an understanding of what Freud is saying in its strongest and most coherent formulation. This is the limited but complex task that I have set out to accomplish in this book.

When I completed my initial draft, I sent it to several friends. Their incisive comments and criticisms were more than helpful; they stimulated me to rewrite the entire draft. I have not answered all of their objections, but I am confident that this is now a much better book as a result of their perceptive criticisms. I am especially grateful for the care taken by colleagues from such diverse disciplines: Carol Bernstein (literary theory); Edward Casey (philosophy); Louise Kaplan (psychoanalysis); Wayne Proudfoot (religious studies); Joel Whitebook (philosophy and psychoanalysis); Nicholas Wolterstorff (philosophy and philosophical theology); and Eli Zaretsky (history). I also want to thank my research assistant, Lynne Taddeo, for her care and good judgment in preparing my manuscript for publication.

Assmann tells us that once he started writing his book, he could not set it aside to work on other projects until he had completed his final draft. He speaks of the Moses discourse as having a life of its own. I too have experienced this compelling power. I am sure that Freud would have profoundly understood this.

Abbreviations

WORKS BY SIGMUND FREUD

MM	*Der Mann Moses und die Monotheistische Religion*
TT	*Totem and Taboo*
SFAZ	*The Letters of Sigmund Freud and Arnold Zweig*
SFLA	*Sigmund Freud and Lou Andreas-Salomé: Letters*

SECONDARY WORKS

AF	*Archive Fever: A Freudian Impression*, by Jacques Derrida
FM	*Freud's Moses: Judaism Terminable and Interminable*, by Yosef Hayim Yerushalmi
HN	*"Freud on the Historical Novel,"* by Yosef Hayim Yerushalmi
J	*The Life and Work of Sigmund Freud*, by Ernest Jones
ME	*Moses the Egyptian: The Memory of Egypt in Western Monotheism*, by Jan Assmann
MFMS	*"The Moses of Freud and the Moses of Schoenberg,"* by Yosef Hayim Yerushalmi
Z	*Zakhor: Jewish History and Jewish Memory*, by Yosef Hayim Yerushalmi

CHAPTER I

The Egyptian origin of monotheism and the murder of Moses

PROLOGUE

In December 1930, Sigmund Freud wrote a short, but remarkable preface for the Hebrew translation of *Totem and Taboo*.

No reader of [the Hebrew version of] this book will find it easy to put himself in the emotional position of an author who is ignorant of the language of holy writ, who is completely estranged from the religion of his fathers – as well as from every other religion – and who cannot take a share in nationalist ideals, but who has yet never repudiated his people, who feels that he is in his essential nature a Jew and who has no desire to alter that nature. If the question were put to him: 'Since you have abandoned all these common characteristics of your countrymen, what is there left to you that is Jewish?' he would reply: 'A very great deal, and *probably its very essence*.' He could not now express that essence clearly in words; but some day, no doubt, it will become accessible to the scientific mind.

Thus it is an experience of a quite special kind for such an author when a book of his is translated into the Hebrew language and put into the hands of readers for whom that historic idiom is a living tongue: a book, moreover, which deals with the origin of religion and morality, though it adopts no Jewish standpoint and makes no exceptions in favour of Jewry. The author hopes, however, that he will be at one with his readers in the conviction that unprejudiced science cannot remain a stranger to the spirit of the new Jewry. (Vienna, *December* 1930)[1]

Like so much of Freud's prose, this passage is at once seemingly straightforward, elusive, and provocative. What does it mean when Freud affirms that he is in his *essential* nature a Jew even though he is estranged from "the religion of his fathers – as well as from religion"? What does it mean to suggest that this essence will someday "become accessible to the scientific mind"? One reason why this preface is so provocative is because Freud succinctly affirms what many godless secular Jews want to affirm – that even though they reject the religion of their fathers, they are nevertheless, in essence, Jews. Yet it seems extraordinarily paradoxical to say that one is completely estranged from the religion of his fathers and yet "feels" that one is a Jew in "his essential nature." Can one so neatly and rigorously distinguish the religion of Judaism from the essential nature of Jewishness? Our perplexity is increased when we realize that the book, *Totem and Taboo*, for which this preface was written, never mentions Judaism, Jews, or Jewishness.

Did Freud ever answer – or even seek to answer – the question he raises about the essential nature of being a Jew? Did he really think that such an answer "will become accessible to the scientific mind"? The thesis that I want to explore and defend in this book is that Freud did attempt to answer these questions. This attempt is found most explicitly in *The Man Moses and the Monotheistic Religion*,[2] a book that has troubled and offended many of his commentators; one that is awkwardly and hesitantly written; a book that many have taken to be written when Freud as an old man was losing his creative powers; a book whose historical claims seem like pure phantasy – where Freud builds "a magnificent castle in the air";[3] a book that many have read as an expression of Freud's alleged Jewish self-hatred. My thesis may itself seem paradoxical, especially in the light of the opening sentence of the book: "To deprive a people of the man whom they take pride in as the greatest of their sons is not a thing to be gladly or carelessly undertaken, least of all by someone who is himself one of them" (23:7).

The grounds for the plausibility of my thesis have already been prepared by the illuminating interpretations of Yosef Yerushalmi, Jan Assmann, and Jacques Derrida.[4] They have offered much more subtle, imaginative readings of what is surely one of Freud's strangest books. Although I will not explore all of the by-paths which they open (and will indicate where I depart from them), I want to acknowledge my enormous debt to their fresh perspectives.

But first, an anticipation and a warning. When Freud indicates that the essence of Jewishness "will become accessible to the scientific mind," and closes his preface by declaring "that unprejudiced science cannot remain a stranger to the spirit of the new Jewry" he is referring to psychoanalysis as a science. Freud strongly believed that we will never fully understand the phenomenon of religion (and Judaism in particular) without appealing to the insights achieved by the new science of psychoanalysis. But Freud avoids any suggestion of vulgar reductionism. He is explicit and emphatic in maintaining that there is not a single causal explanation or single origin for religious phenomena. He begins the fourth essay of *Totem and Taboo* (where he advances the hypothesis that "totemic religion" originates when the "brothers who had been driven out came together, killed and devoured their father and so made an end of the patriarchal horde") by declaring:

There are no grounds for fearing that psycho-analysis, which first discovered that psychical acts and structures are invariably over-determined, will be tempted to trace the origin of anything so complicated as religion to a single source. If psycho-analysis is compelled – and is, indeed, in duty bound – to lay all the emphasis upon one particular source, that does not mean it is claiming either that that source is the only one or that it occupies first place among the numerous contributory factors. Only when we can synthesize the findings in the different fields of research will it become possible to arrive at the relative importance of the part played in the genesis of religion by the mechanism discussed in these pages. Such a task lies beyond the means as well as beyond the purposes of a psycho-analyst. (13:100)

There is a temptation, especially when considering the question of Freud's Jewishness and the significance of his *Moses* (as the last book that he published), to apply the concepts of psychoanalysis to Freud himself. Some commentators have sought to put Freud "on the couch." They speculate about the relationship between Freud and his father Jacob, and the relationship between Freud's claims about the Jewish people and their father figure, Moses. I strongly believe that such a temptation should be resisted. Freud himself frequently refers to his arguments in the three essays that comprise *The Man Moses and the Monotheistic Religion*. What precisely are these claims and arguments? Are they persuasive? Because Freud's assertions are (at times) apparently far-fetched or even repugnant, commentators have been too quick to search for hidden meanings and extraneous accounts for *why* Freud says what he does. The first task of a commentator is to pay careful attention to what is being said, and to do justice to the nature of the explicit claims and arguments of the text. This is why I will quote extensively from Freud's text, and follow the exposition of Freud's arguments. Furthermore, such a close reading will occasionally require repeating key passages from Freud's work in order to bring out their full significance.

In his classic study, *Freud and Philosophy*, Paul Ricoeur introduced his now famous distinction between two extreme styles of hermeneutics – a reductive and demystifying hermeneutics, a hermeneutics of suspicion; and a non-reductive and restorative hermeneutics, a hermeneutics of trust.[5] Given these extremes, there has been a tendency (especially in dealing with Freud's *Moses*) to approach this text from the perspective of the hermeneutics of suspicion. But Ricoeur himself emphatically makes the point (which has been too frequently ignored) that there is a subtle dialectical relation between these extremes. They are mutually dependent. We cannot even begin the process of demystification unless we pay careful attention to what is manifest. This is what is required if we are to try to decipher and demystify a text. There are many places where Freud's arguments are open to serious – even devastating – criticism, and I will not hesitate to indicate them. But the primary stance that I have adopted in this study is to follow the hermeneutical principle of presenting the strongest possible case for Freud. I have done this not because I agree with him, or because I find his characterization of the essence of Jewishness fully persuasive, but because I am convinced that the power and significance of Freud's claims about religion, tradition, Jewishness, and Jewish survival have not yet been fully drawn out and confronted.

THE NARRATIVE PLOT

Yerushalmi has given an eloquent summary of the bare plot of Freud's Moses. In order to orient my own inquiry, I begin by quoting this summary:

Monotheism is not of Jewish origin but an Egyptian discovery. The pharaoh Amenhotep IV established it as his state religion in the form of an exclusive worship of the sun-power, or Aton, thereafter calling himself Ikhnaton. The Aton religion, according to Freud, was characterized by the exclusive belief in one God, the rejection of anthropomorphism, magic, and sorcery, and the absolute denial of an afterlife. Upon Ikhnaton's death, however, his great heresy was rapidly undone, and the Egyptians reverted to their old gods. Moses was not a Hebrew but an Egyptian priest or noble, and a fervent monotheist. In order to save the Aton religion from extinction he placed himself at the head of an oppressed Semitic tribe then living in Egypt, brought them forth from bondage, and created a new nation. He gave them an even more spiritualized, imageless form of monotheistic religion and, in order to set them apart, introduced the Egyptian custom of circumcision. But the crude mass of former slaves could not bear the severe demands of the new faith. In a mob revolt Moses was killed and the memory of the murder repressed. The Israelites went on to forge an alliance of compromise with kindred Semitic tribes in Midian whose fierce volcanic deity, named Yahweh, now became their national god. As a result, the god of Moses was fused with Yahweh and the deeds of Moses ascribed to a Midianite priest also called Moses. However, over a period of centuries the submerged tradition of the true faith and its founder gathered sufficient force to reassert itself and emerge victorious. Yahweh was henceforth endowed with the universal and spiritual qualities of Moses' god, though the memory of Moses' murder remained repressed among the Jews, reemerging only in a very disguised form with the rise of Christianity. (*FM*, 3 – 4)[6]

At first glance (and even at second or third glance) this narrative seems so fantastic that it is difficult to take it seriously as an historical account. One may be inclined to think that this is nothing but a pure fiction or phantasy with little or no basis in historical fact, and that the only interesting question is what possibly could have motivated Freud to tell such a shocking tale – one which could (and did) offend his fellow Jews. For despite the pleas of some Jewish scholars to suppress publishing this book, Freud published it during one of the darkest and most threatening periods in Jewish history.

Although this is the bare plot of the story that Freud tells, it is not the way in which he tells it. We need to pay close attention to *how* Freud tells his tale. The first two essays of the three that comprise the book, "Moses an Egyptian" and "If Moses was an Egyptian . . .," originally appeared in the psychoanalytic journal, *Imago*, when Freud was still living in Vienna. The third, the longest and most substantial essay, "Moses, His People and Monotheist Religion," was only published in 1939 after Freud's arrival in England.

THE HYPOTHESIS: MOSES WAS AN EGYPTIAN

"Moses an Egyptian," a short (eight pages in the original German), modest essay focuses on the question of whether Moses was an Egyptian. Freud does not even discuss monotheism in this essay, although he does say that the man Moses "set the Jewish people free" and "gave them their laws and founded their religion" (23:7). To support the hypothesis that Moses was an Egyptian, Freud begins by citing those authorities (primarily J.H. Breasted) who claimed that "Moses" was an Egyptian name. Freud suggests that the authorities who traced the etymology of "Moses" to its Egyptian sources should "at least have considered the possibility that the person who bore this Egyptian name may himself have been an Egyptian" (23:9). This is a rather thin reed to support a serious historical claim, especially when we realize that throughout their history Jews have adopted names from the places in which they have been living. Furthermore, according to the biblical narrative (the primary source for our knowledge of Moses), it is the

Egyptian Princess who discovers the infant, and brings him up. It makes good sense that a child in the Egyptian royal court would have an Egyptian name. So the question arises: does Freud himself have any fresh arguments to support his controversial hypothesis? He believes that he does, but before proceeding, he tells us that what he has to contribute is an "application of psycho-analysis," and the "argument" arrived at in this way "will undoubtedly only impress that minority of readers who are familiar with analytic thinking and who are able to appreciate its findings" (23:10).

Freud begins his argument by considering *The Myth of the Birth of the Hero*, a book published by Otto Rank in 1909 ("who was at that time still under my influence" [23:10]). Rank calls our attention to the "baffling similarity" in the narrative structure of the legends and poetic tales that glorify the origins of national heroes, founders of religions, dynasties, empires, or cities. Rank's researches make us acquainted with the source and purpose of these myths. "A hero is someone who has had the courage to rebel against his father and in the end victoriously overcome him" (23:12). Presenting a generalized picture of this myth, Freud isolates a number of common features: a child's birth by aristocratic parents; his conception preceded by difficulties; condemning the (male) child to death or exposure by his father; the child's rescue by animals or by a humble family; the adventures of the child as he grows up and discovers who his parents really are; the revenge he takes against his father; and finally his achievement of greatness and fame. From a psychoanalytic perspective, this myth has the generalized structure of the "family romance" – "the source of the whole poetic fiction" (23:12).[7]

But what precisely does this have to do with Moses being an Egyptian? Freud himself calls our attention to a glaring contradiction between the structure of this exposure myth and the biblical account of Moses' birth. In the generalized exposure narrative the "real" parents of the hero are aristocratic, and those who save him from death are quite humble. But Moses, the child of Jewish parents who were slaves in Egypt, is saved by the royal princess, and is brought up as a member of an aristocratic Egyptian family. How is this disparity, this contradiction to be explained? Freud lamely suggests that "we are in fact free to suppose that some later and clumsy adapter of the material of the legend found an opportunity for introducing into the story of his hero Moses something which resembled the classical exposure legends marking out a hero, but which, on account of the special circumstances of the case, was not applicable to Moses" (23:14). Freud seems to acknowledge how flimsy this argument really is, for he tells us: "Our investigations might have had to rest content with this inconclusive and, moreover, uncertain outcome, and they might have done nothing towards answering the question of whether Moses was an Egyptian" (23:14).

But Freud does not leave us with this "uncertain outcome." He suggests that there is "another and perhaps more hopeful line of approach to an assessment of the legend of exposure" (23:14). According to the analytic interpretation, the two families in the myth (aristocratic and humble) are really identical. When this myth is told about historical persons, then "[o]ne of the families is the real one, in which the person in question (the great man) was actually born and grew up; the other is fictitious, fabricated by the myth in pursuit of its own intentions. As a rule the humble family is the real one and the aristocratic family the fabricated one" (23:14). If we strictly followed the logic of Freud's reasoning, then this pattern would accord with the way in which the biblical story of Moses is actually told. Moses' real parents were humble Jews. But Freud makes a curious, wildly speculative leap when he says:

in every instance which it has been possible to test [Freud does not specify any instances, nor does he indicate what constitutes a test – RJB], the first family, the one from which the child was exposed, was the invented one, and the second one, in which he was received and grew up, was the real one. If we have the courage to recognize this assertion as universally true and as applying also to the legend of Moses, then all at once we see things clearly: Moses was an Egyptian – probably an aristocrat – whom the legend was designed to turn into a Jew. And that would be our conclusion. (23:15)

It is difficult to know whether one is expected to take any of this seriously – even as an application of psychoanalysis. An ungenerous reader might even say it sounds more like a *reductio ad absurdum*. At almost every stage in his argument Freud makes all sorts of unwarranted and speculative assumptions.

Freud concludes this first short essay by raising the very question his readers will surely ask: "If no more certainty could be reached than this, why, it may be asked, have I brought this enquiry into public notice at all?" (23:16). Why, indeed! Freud hints about what is to come, but refrains from explicitly telling us:

For if one allows oneself to be carried away by the two arguments which I have put forward here, and if one sets out to take the hypothesis seriously that Moses was an aristocratic Egyptian, very interesting and far-reaching prospects are opened up. With the help of some not very remote assumptions, we shall, I believe, be able to understand the motives which led Moses in the unusual step he took and, closely related to this, to obtain a grasp of the possible basis of a number of the characteristics and peculiarities of the laws and religion which he gave to the Jewish people; and we shall even be led on to important considerations regarding the origin of monotheist religions in general. (23:16)

These are extraordinary hints. Freud seductively arouses our curiosity, but refuses to tell us anything more in this essay. Psychological probabilities are not enough to justify such consequential historical claims, and there is a paucity of objective evidence about the period in which Moses lived. In the final sentence of this essay, Freud tells us that because such objective evidence "has not been obtainable . . . it will therefore be better to leave unmentioned any further implications of the discovery that Moses was an Egyptian" (23:16).[8] Freud's readers had to wait several months for the next installment to find out what he meant by the hints that he dropped at the end of his essay. Significantly, this next installment was entitled "If Moses was an Egyptian . . ." The most significant part of this title is the ellipsis.

Before proceeding in our examination of his text, it is worth asking: why did Freud publish this brief and inconclusive essay? This work does not make any significant historical contribution, nor does it add anything substantial to our understanding of psychoanalysis. We know that Freud was genuinely apprehensive about publishing his hypothesis concerning Moses' birth – and not only because he felt that there was so little "objective evidence" to support his claim. The circumspection of his first essay seems to have been a way of getting a hearing for the conjecture that Moses was an Egyptian, without, however, providing any clear indication of the inferences that Freud was to draw from this conjecture. In a sense, Freud (because he already knew what he was holding back) was cautiously "testing the waters."

THE ELLIPSIS: IF MOSES WAS AN EGYPTIAN . . .

It is only in his second essay, "If Moses Was An Egyptian . . .," that the full drama of the historical plot is revealed. This essay does read like a precis of a "historical novel," in which the dramatic climax is reached when the Semites, whom the Egyptian Moses had led out of Egypt, slay him. Despite the shocking (and for a religious believer – Jew or Christian – the blasphemous) claims that Freud makes, he begins by speaking of his hesitations and conflicting motives in publishing his views. "The greater the importance of the views arrived at in this way [basing them on 'psychological probabilities'], the more strongly one feels the need to beware of exposing them without a secure basis to the critical assaults of the world around one – like a bronze statue with feet of clay" (23:17). It may jolt us (we will return to this statement) when Freud announces: "But once again this is not the whole story nor *the most important part* of the whole story" (23:17, emphasis added).

Considering that this essay was published in 1937, on the eve of one of the darkest periods of Jewish history, the very way in which Freud goes about narrating his historical reconstruction could scarcely avoid causing offense and anguish to his fellow Jews. In his opening paragraph, he makes a derogatory reference to those "[t]almudists who delight in exhibiting their ingenuity without regard to how remote from reality their thesis may be" (23:17). Freud seems to be anticipating and defending himself against the very charge that would be brought against him. As he begins exploring the implications of the hypothesis that Moses was an Egyptian, he characterizes the Semites (the Jews who were living in Egypt at the time of Moses) as follows:

But it is not easy to guess what could induce an aristocratic Egyptian [Moses] – a prince, perhaps, or a priest or high official – to put himself at the head of *a crowd of immigrant foreigners at a backward level of civilization* and to leave his country with them. (23:18, emphasis added)

The most striking characteristic of the second essay, "If Moses Was An Egyptian . . .," is that it reads like a "purely historical study" (23:52) of what presumably really happened. Freud does not explicitly refer to psychoanalysis. On the contrary, he deliberately restrains himself from offering any psychoanalytic interpretations, even when the subject being discussed clearly invites such interpretations (for example, his discussion of circumcision). I suspect that if this essay had been published anonymously, a reader might have thought it was the work of a crackpot who invented an intriguing tale of how the Egyptian aristocrat, Moses, forced his adopted monotheistic religion upon the savage Semites who "took fate into their own hands and rid themselves of their tyrant [Moses]" (23:47). Freud refers selectively to the works of historians and biblical scholars (choosing those sources he can use to support his thesis that Moses was an Egyptian). He plays fast and loose with what he selects and uses from the Bible. He cavalierly justifies this practice in the following footnote:

I am very well aware that in dealing so autocratically and arbitrarily with Biblical tradition – bringing it up to confirm my views when it suits me and unhesitatingly rejecting it when it contradicts me – I am exposing myself to serious methodological criticism and weakening the convincing force of my arguments. But this is the only way in which one can treat material of which one knows definitely that its trustworthiness has been severely impaired by the distorting influence of tendentious purposes. It is to be hoped that I shall find some degree of justification later on, when I come upon the track of these secret motives. Certainty is in any case unattainable and moreover it may be said that every other writer on the subject has adopted the same procedure. (23:27)

Why does Freud – who initially, in his first essay, describes his contribution as an "application of psycho-analysis" – now completely bracket the question of psychoanalysis and adopt the mantle of the scholarly historian who is seeking to establish what really happened in fourteenth century BCE? We find a clue if we go back to his first essay. Freud's main argument in support of the hypothesis that Moses was an Egyptian depended on his psychoanalytic interpretation of the exposure myth of national heroes. Freud claims that recognizable fragments of this myth are found in the legends of Sargon of Agade, Moses, Cyrus, Romulus, Oedipus, Karna, Paris, Telephos, Perseus, Heracles, Gilgamesh, Amphion, and Zethos. Note that this list consists primarily of *mythological* figures. But according to Freud, the Egyptian Moses was a *real* person who lived at a precise historical time; adopted the monotheistic religion from the Egyptian Pharaoh, Akhenaton; and, in order to save the Aton religion, forced it upon the Semites living in Egypt. Without establishing these "historical" facts, Freud would have *no* basis for the psychoanalytic interpretation that he eventually offers to explain these "facts."

If we look back to the final paragraph of "Moses An Egyptian," we will see that Freud has already indicated this need for historical evidence:

Even if one accepts the fact of Moses being an Egyptian as a first historical foothold, one would need to have at least a second firm fact in order to defend the wealth of emerging possibilities against the criticism of their being a product of the imagination and too remote from reality. (23:16)

Moreover, at the beginning of "Moses An Egyptian," Freud discusses the need to establish the basic "historical" facts about Moses. "It is justly argued that the later history of the people of Israel would be incomprehensible if this premiss [that Moses was a real person and that the Exodus from Egypt associated with him did in fact take place] were not accepted" (23:7).

Although Freud repeatedly tells us that there can be no certainty about what really happened in Egypt and the Exodus into the wilderness, he does not seem to have any *serious* doubts that the events he describes actually happened. There is a slippery slide in his prose from imaginative conjecture to established conclusion. For example, in the final sentence of his first essay he no longer speaks of his "hypothesis" that Moses was an Egyptian, but rather of "the *discovery* that Moses was an Egyptian" (23:16, emphasis added). In the opening paragraph of the second essay, where Freud recapitulates his "fresh argument" in support of the claim that Moses was an Egyptian, he now says: "What I added was that the interpretation of the myth of exposure which was linked with Moses *necessarily* led to the inference that he was an Egyptian whom the needs of a people sought to make into a Jew" (23:17, emphasis added).

The more closely we examine the details of Freud's narrative of what supposedly really happened, the more outrageous it appears. There are all sorts of gaps, leaps, dubious assumptions, and wild guesses. For example, the Bible tells us very little about the origins of the Levites who play such an important role in the Exodus story (and in Jewish history). Freud himself acknowledges that "[o]ne of the greatest enigmas of Jewish prehistory is that of the origin of the Levites . . . one of the twelve tribes of Israel" (23:38). But Freud thinks he can solve this enigma. He proposes this solution:

It is incredible that a great lord, like Moses the Egyptian, should have joined this alien people unaccompanied. He certainly must have brought a retinue with him – his closest followers, his scribes, his domestic servants. This is who the Levites originally were. The tradition which alleges that Moses was a Levite seems to be a clear distortion of the fact: the Levites were the [Egyptian] followers of Moses. This solution is supported by the fact . . . that it is only among the Levites that Egyptian names occur later. (23:38)

So when it is declared in the Book of Exodus that Moses came down from Sinai and saw his people worshipping the golden calf, the sons of Levi who followed Moses' command and slaughtered "three thousand men" were really Moses' Egyptian retinue! (However, in Freud's historical reconstruction, the Egyptian Moses was never even at Sinai. And Freud does not believe that Aaron ever existed.)

If we accept Freud's claim that it really was the Egyptian Moses who imposed the monotheistic religion upon the hapless Semites, then we may well ask, how are we to account for the biblical references to the patriarchs: Abraham, Isaac, and Jacob? Consider Freud's tortuous explanation.

It was at Kadesh, an oasis in the desert, where the Semites who had already murdered their Egyptian leader, Moses, joined with other tribes who worshipped a different god, the Midianite volcanic god, Yahweh – "[a] coarse, narrow-minded, local god, violent and bloodthirsty" (23:50). There was now a need to glorify this new god, to work out some sort of compromise so that Yahweh – the fierce demon god – would "fit" with the monotheistic god that the Egyptian Semites worshipped. Consequently, in working out this compromise, the "legends of the patriarchs of the people – Abraham, Isaac and Jacob – were introduced. Yahweh asserted that he was already the god of these forefathers; though it is true that he himself had to admit that they had not worshipped him under that name" (23:44). This was done for the "tendentious purpose" of glorifying the volcanic god, Yahweh, and fusing him with the monotheistic god of the Egyptian Moses.

We can now better understand the significance of what Freud wrote at the very beginning of his first essay. "The man Moses, who set the Jewish people free, who gave them their laws and *founded their religion*, dates from such remote times that we cannot evade a preliminary enquiry as to whether he was a historical personage or a creature of legend" (23:7, emphasis added). It is not God, or even Abraham, Isaac, and Jacob, who founded the religion of the Jewish people. It is the *man* Moses who founded their religion. It is not God (either the monotheistic god of Moses or the demon god of the Midianites, Yahweh) who chose the Jewish people. It is Moses who *chose* the Jews to be the worshippers of the monotheistic god, Aten. "Moses had stooped to the Jews, had made them his people: they were his 'chosen people'" (23:45). Freud does not tell us what the religion of the Jewish Semites living in Egypt was *before* Moses chose them for his monotheistic religion, but he clearly indicates that it was not any form of monotheism.

Yerushalmi, in his plot summary, tells us that Moses gave the Semites "an even more spiritualized, imageless form of monotheistic religion and, in order to set them apart, introduced the Egyptian custom of circumcision" (*FM*, 3). This almost casual reference to the Egyptian custom of circumcision scarcely does justice to the crucial role that it plays in "If Moses was an Egyptian . . ." Freud refers to the evidence afforded by circumcision as a "key-fossil" which has "repeatedly been of help to us" (23:39). If one is aware of the psychoanalytic interpretation(s) of circumcision and its close association with castration – as certainly most of Freud's readers of his essay would be – then we might think that here we will finally discover the opening for a psychoanalytic interpretation of Freud's historical reconstruction. But once again we are disappointed. There is no mention of castration in this essay. Freud restricts himself to the *conscious* motives that Moses had in circumcising the "backward" Semites. It is, so Freud claims, an established fact that circumcision was an Egyptian custom. In order to insure that the chosen Semites would not feel inferior to the Egyptians, Moses introduced the custom of circumcision.

We are familiar with the attitude adopted by people (both nations and individuals) to this primaeval usage, which is scarcely understood any longer. Those who do not practise it look on it as very strange and are a little horrified by it, but those who have adopted circumcision are proud of it. They feel exalted by it, ennobled, as it were, and look down with contempt on the others, whom they regard as unclean . . . It may be supposed that Moses, who, being an Egyptian, was himself circumcised, shared this attitude. The Jews with whom he departed from his country were to serve him as a superior substitute for the Egyptians he had left behind. On no account must the Jews be inferior to them. He wished to make them into a 'holy nation', as is expressly stated in the biblical text, and as a mark of this consecration he introduced among them too the custom which made them at least the equals of the Egyptians. And he could only welcome it if they were to be isolated by such a sign and kept apart from the foreign peoples among whom their wanderings would lead them, just as Egyptians themselves had kept apart from all foreigners. (23:29–30)

Here Freud does use, as partial support for his explanation of the introduction of circumcision, the biblical text. For this is the way he interprets the phrase from Exodus about making the Israelites into a "holy nation." But then we may ask: what does Freud say about the more traditional interpretation of circumcision as a sign of the covenant between God and Abraham – as a physical mark of the covenant between God and the Jewish people? He categorically denigrates and dismisses this tradition.

Moses did not only give the Jews a new religion; it can be stated with equal certainty that he introduced the custom of circumcision to them. This *fact* is of decisive importance for our problem and has scarcely ever been considered. It is true that the Biblical account contradicts this more than once. On the one hand it traces circumcision back to the patriarchal age as a mark of a covenant between God and Abraham; on the other hand it describes in a quite particularly obscure passage how God was angry with Moses for having neglected a custom which had become holy, and sought to kill him; but that his wife, a Midianite, saved her husband from God's wrath by quickly performing the operation. These, however, are distortions, which should not lead us astray; later on we shall discover the reason for them. The fact remains that *there is only one answer to the question of where the Jews derived the custom of circumcision from – namely, from Egypt.* (23:26 – 7, emphasis added)

Perhaps Freud's most ingenious account of circumcision is to show that this custom provides us with a further proof that Moses was an Egyptian. Freud argues as follows:

Herodotus, the 'father of history', tells us that the custom of circumcision had long been indigenous in Egypt, and his statements are confirmed by the findings in mummies and indeed by pictures on the walls of tombs. No other people of the Eastern Mediterranean, so far as we know, practised this custom; it may safely be presumed that the Semites, Babylonians and Sumerians were uncircumcised. The Bible story itself says this is so of the inhabitants of Canaan; it is a necessary premiss to the adventure of Jacob's daughter and the prince of Shechem. The possibility that the Jews acquired the custom of circumcision during their sojourn in Egypt in some way other than in connection with the religious teaching of Moses may be rejected as completely without foundation. Now, taking it as certain that circumcision was a universal popular custom in Egypt, let us for a moment adopt the ordinary hypothesis that Moses was a Jew, who sought to free his compatriots from bondage in Egypt and lead them to develop an independent and self-conscious national existence in another country – which was what in fact happened. What sense could it have, in that case, that he should at the same time impose on them a troublesome custom which even, to some extent, made them into Egyptians and which must keep permanently alive their memory of Egypt – whereas his efforts could only be aimed in the opposite direction, towards alienating his people from the land of their bondage and overcoming their longing for the 'flesh-pots of Egypt'? No, the fact from which we started and the hypothesis which we added to it are so incompatible with each other that we may be bold enough to reach this conclusion: if Moses gave the Jews not only a new religion but also the commandment for circumcision, he was not a Jew but an Egyptian, and in that case the Mosaic religion was probably an Egyptian one and, in view of its contrast to the popular religion, the religion of the Aten, with which the later Jewish religion agrees in some remarkable respects. (23:27 – 8)

We may feel uneasy about the way in which Freud so freely appeals to the Hebrew Bible when it suits his purposes, and dismisses it as a distortion when it contradicts his beliefs. Freud does open himself to serious methodological critique when he self-confidently asserts: "No historian can regard the biblical account of Moses and the Exodus as anything other than a pious piece of imaginative fiction, which has recast a remote tradition for the benefit of its own tendentious purposes" (23:33). It is never quite clear what Freud's criterion is for selecting those features of the biblical account which he takes to be reliable indicators of the historical truth and those which he tells us are distortions. It is difficult to resist the conclusion that once Freud became convinced about what he thought really happened, he then scanned the Bible in order to select the evidence that would support his case. Throughout this second essay Freud repeats the charge that the pious scribes who wrote and edited the biblical account (centuries after the events occurred) had "tendentious purposes." But he never even acknowledges that, despite his pose of being the disinterested historian seeking to establish the objective facts, he might also be accused of harboring such "tendentious purposes."

I do think we can understand – although not *justify* – what Freud is doing in these essays. Suppose, for the sake of argument, we adopt the hypothesis that Freud had somehow guessed the truth of what really happened when Moses took the Jews out of Egypt into the wilderness. If the Egyptian Semites murdered Moses, then it seems to make sense that the scribes who authored and edited the Pentateuch would want to conceal this fact. They would seek to eliminate its traces from the biblical narrative.9 We can appreciate the significance of Freud's famous analogy between a murder and a distortion of a text.

In its implications the distortion of a text resembles a murder: the difficulty is not in perpetrating the deed, but in getting rid of its traces. We might well lend the word '*Entstellung* [distortion]' the double meaning to which it has a claim but of which to-day it makes no use. It should mean not only 'to change the appearance of something' but also 'to put something in another place, to displace'. Accordingly, in many instances of textual distortion, we may nevertheless count upon finding what has been suppressed and disavowed hidden away somewhere else, though changed and torn from its context. Only it will not always be easy to recognize it. (23:43)

The analogy that Freud draws between the distortion of a text and a murder is used to characterize the (alleged) textual distortion of the murder of Moses. Because the pious biblical scribes tried to conceal the murder of Moses, then the task of the (psychoanalytic) detective historian is to discover those traces of the murder that have not been completely obliterated.

But we can also apply this analogy to Freud's own text – a text in which there are also "almost everywhere noticeable gaps, disturbing repetitions and obvious contradictions" (23:43). What is being distorted and concealed here? Is Freud himself changing "the appearance of something" and putting "something in another place"? We have good

reasons for thinking that there is a distortion (*Entstellung*) when we recall
that Freud began this essay by affirming "But once again this is not the
whole story nor the most important part of the whole story" (23:17).
What is the whole story? Do we find traces in this essay of the most
important part of the whole story?

We will not be able to answer these questions adequately until we
consider the third and most substantial essay, "Moses, his People and
Monotheist Religion." But I want to step back and reflect on the first
two essays – the essays published when Freud was still living in Vienna,
with an acute awareness of the ominous threats to European Jewry (and
to the discipline of psychoanalysis).

Let us put aside our doubts and reservations, and assume that what
Freud has related is more or less historically accurate. What has Freud
established? This is his own concise summary:

And here, it seems, I have reached the conclusion of my study, which was
directed to the single aim of introducing the figure of an Egyptian Moses into the
nexus of Jewish history. Our findings may be thus expressed in the most concise
formula. Jewish history is familiar to us for its dualities: *two* groups of people who
came together to form the nation, *two* kingdoms into which this nation fell apart,
two gods' names in the documentary sources of the Bible. To these we add two
fresh ones: the foundation of *two* religions – the first repressed by the second but
nevertheless later emerging victoriously behind it, and *two* religious founders,
who are both called by the same name of Moses and whose personalities we
have to distinguish from each other. All of these dualities are the necessary
consequences of the first one: the fact that one portion of the people had an
experience which must be regarded as traumatic and which the other portion
escaped. Beyond this there would be a very great deal to discuss, to explain and
to assert. Only thus would an interest in our purely historical study find its true
justification. What the real nature of a tradition resides in, and what its special
power rests on, how impossible it is to dispute the personal influence upon
world-history of individual great men, what sacrilege one commits against the
splendid diversity of human life if one recognizes only those motives which arise
from material needs, from what sources some ideas (and particularly religious
ones) derive their power to subject both men and peoples to their yoke – to study
all this in the special case of Jewish history would be an alluring task. To
continue my work on such lines as these would be to find a link with the
statements I put forward twenty-five years ago in *Totem and Taboo* [1912 – 1913].
But I no longer feel that I have the strength to do so. (23:52 – 3)

This is an eloquent, moving, and elusive conclusion. Freud does not
explicitly mention the murder of Moses. He only refers to it indirectly:
"one portion of the people had an experience which must be regarded

as traumatic." We might even feel that there is a parallel between Freud and the biblical Moses – the Moses who leads the Israelites to the promised land, but does not enter it. This conclusion is also filled with promises – promises which the aged and dying Freud might never have fulfilled. Thus far Freud has told us a likely story, but its significance, especially its psychoanalytic meaning, has not been made explicit. Freud tells us that there is still a "great deal to discuss" – and only in light of this would "our purely historical study find its true justification."

Let us also recall that at the end of his first essay, Freud indicated that if we "take the hypothesis seriously that Moses was an aristocratic Egyptian," we would be able "to obtain a grasp of the possible basis of a number of the characteristics and peculiarities of the laws and religion which he gave to the Jewish people; and we shall even be led on to important considerations regarding the origin of monotheist religions in general" (23:16). But thus far Freud has not fulfilled this promise. What do the alleged historical events of the middle of the fourteenth century BCE have to do with the Jewish people today? And how does all this bear on the thesis that I announced at the beginning – that in *The Man Moses and the Monotheistic Religion* we will discover Freud's attempt to answer the question: what is the essence of (his) Jewishness? It is only by examining the final essay that we will be able to answer these questions, but I do think that we can begin to discern traces of Freud's answer.

MOSAIC MONOTHEISM: INITIAL HINTS

In order to show that there are already indications of Freud's answer, I want to raise a fundamental question about Freud's historical account which I have not yet directly considered. If the Egyptian Semites rose up and killed their leader Moses, what were their motives? Why did the Jews murder Moses? To answer this question, we need to examine Freud's understanding of the monotheistic religion that the Jews had thrust upon them. Throughout his second essay (and even more explicitly in the third essay) there is a subtle but very revealing valorization of the superior "spiritual and intellectual" (*geistig*) significance of monotheism over more "primitive" forms of polytheism.[10] Let us review some of the details of Freud's historical account of the origin of the Aten religion in Egypt and how it is related to Jewish monotheism.

The "Jewish religion which is attributed to Moses" is a "rigid monotheism on the grand scale: there is only one God, he is the sole God, omnipotent, unapproachable; his aspect is more than human eyes can tolerate, no image must be made of him, even his name may not be spoken" (23:18). Freud initially presents this characterization as an obstacle to his claim that the Jewish religion was originally an Egyptian religion. For prior to Akhenaten, the Egyptian religion was an "unrestricted" and "primitive" polytheism. There is a "violent contrast" (23:18) between the Mosaic religion and Egyptian polytheism.

In the Egyptian religion there is an almost innumerable host of deities of varying dignity and origin: a few personifications of great natural forces such as heaven and earth, sun and moon, an occasional abstraction such as Ma'at (truth or justice) or a caricature such as the dwarf-like Bes; but most of them local gods, dating from the period when the country was divided into numerous provinces, with the shape of animals, as though they had not yet completed their evolution from the old totem animals, with no sharp distinctions between them, and scarcely differing in the functions allotted to them. (23:18 – 19)

But the Mosaic religion condemns magic and sorcery in the severest terms, and there is a "harsh prohibition against making an image of any living or imagined creature." In Egyptian polytheism, magic and sorcery "proliferate with the greatest luxuriance" (23:19). There is an "insatiable appetite of the Egyptians for embodying their gods in clay, stone and metal" (23:19). Furthermore, "the ancient Jewish religion renounced immortality entirely; the possibility of existence continuing after death is nowhere and never mentioned" (23:20). In the Egyptian polytheism "Osiris, the god of the dead, the ruler of this other world, was the most popular and undisputed of all the gods of Egypt" (23:20).

Freud stresses the contrast between Jewish monotheism and Egyptian polytheism in order to indicate what "stands in the way" of his hypothesis that the origin of Jewish monotheism is to be found in Egyptian religion. But this "violent contrast" also serves another purpose – to underscore the revolutionary significance of what the young Pharaoh Amenhotep IV (who changed his name to Akhenaten)[11] sought to introduce "in the glorious Eighteenth Dynasty."

This king set about forcing a new religion on his Egyptian subjects – a religion which ran contrary to their thousands-of-years-old traditions and to all the familiar habits of their lives. It was a strict monotheism, the first attempt of the kind, so far as we know, in the history of the world, and along with the belief in a single god religious intolerance was inevitably born, which had previously been alien to the ancient world and remained so long afterwards. (23:20)[12]

Freud – in an almost quasi-Marxist fashion – relates this development to the spread of the Egyptian empire.

This imperialism was reflected in religion as universalism and monotheism. Since the Pharaoh's responsibilities now embraced not only Egypt but Nubia and Syria as well, deity too was obliged to abandon its national limitation and, just as the Pharaoh was the sole and unrestricted ruler of the world known to the Egyptians, this must also apply to the Egyptians' new deity. (23:21)

Freud also tells us that in the course of Akhenaten's reign, which lasted for seventeen years from 1375 BCE until 1358 BCE "[h]e introduced something new, which for the first time converted the doctrine of a universal god into monotheism – the factor of exclusiveness" (23:22).[13] Freud even attributes a radical transformation of the sun cult of On to Akhenaten.

Amenophis never denied his adherence to the sun cult of On. In the two Hymns to the Aten which have survived in the rock tombs and which were probably composed by him himself, he praises the sun as the creator and preserver of all living things both inside and outside Egypt with an ardour which is not repeated till many centuries later in the Psalms in honour of the Jewish god Yahweh. He was not content, however, with this astonishing anticipation of the scientific discovery of the effect of solar radiation. There is no doubt that he went a step further: that he did not worship the sun as a material object but as the symbol of a divine being whose energy was manifested in its rays. (23:22)[14]

The measures taken by Akhenaten to destroy the traditional Egyptian polytheism and to displace it with a harsh, exclusive, intolerant monotheism eventually "provoked a mood of fanatical vindictiveness among the suppressed priesthood and unsatisfied common people . . ." (23:23). After Akhenaten's death there was a violent reaction and a period of anarchy. The priests of Amun, whom Akhenaten had sought to suppress, gained their revenge. Egyptian polytheism was re-established. And there was now an attempt to obliterate the traces of the Aten religion – Akhenaten's monotheism. This attempt might have been successful, if it were not for Moses who was a follower of the Aten religion. Moses could not expect to survive in Egypt. He needed to "choose" a new people, to lead them out of Egypt in order to insure the survival of the Aten religion. Akhenaten had "alienated his people and let his empire fall to pieces. The more energetic nature of Moses was more at home with the plan of founding a new kingdom, of finding a new people to whom he would present for their worship the religion which Egypt had disdained" (23:28).

Freud's narrative provides the background for understanding why the Jews murdered Moses. Jewish monotheism "behaved in some respects even more harshly than the Egyptian: for instance in forbidding pictorial representations of any kind. The most essential difference is to be seen . . . in the fact that the Jewish religion was entirely without sun worship, in which the Egyptian one still found support" (23:25 – 6).

Ironically, despite Freud's significant departures from the biblical account, in this part of his narrative he can draw some support from the Bible. Throughout the biblical account – not only in the famous story of the golden calf – we hear about the "murmurings" of the Jewish people in the wilderness. On several occasions, the Israelites complained and sought to rebel against Moses. They wanted to return to the "fleshpots of Egypt." What does this desire to return to Egypt mean? According to Freud, it means the desire to be rid of the severe demands of mono-theism and return to Egyptian polytheism.[15] Just as the priests of Amum sought their revenge against Akhenaten, so the Jews who had been forced to leave Egypt and adopt a new, strict, harsh, exclusive mono-theism with rigorous ethical standards, sought their revenge against Moses. But there is one consequential difference. In Egypt the reaction set in *after* the death of Akhenaten. But the Jews did not wait until Moses died; they murdered him. Although Freud cautiously introduces this crucial event, he is bold in the inferences that he draws from it.

[I]n 1922, Ernst Sellin made a discovery which affected our problem decisively. He found in the Prophet Hosea (in the second half of the eighth century BC) unmistakable signs of a tradition to the effect that Moses, the founder of their religion, met with a violent end in a rising of his refractory and stiff-necked people, and that at the same time the religion he had introduced was thrown off. This tradition is not, however, restricted to Hosea; it reappears in most of the later Prophets, and indeed, according to Sellin, became the basis of all the later Messianic expectations. At the end of the Babylonian captivity a hope grew up among the Jewish people that the man who had been so shamefully murdered would return from the dead and would lead his remorseful people, and perhaps not them alone, into the kingdom of lasting bliss. (23:36)

Freud, who is acutely sensitive to the accusation that he is spinning imaginative tales, tells us that he is not in a position to judge whether Sellin has interpreted the biblical passages correctly, but he acknowl-edges that Sellin's hypothesis "allows us to spin our threads further without contradicting the authentic findings of historical research" (23:37). Once again we can detect the slide from conjecture to estab-lished conclusion. Freud begins the seventh (and final section) of "If Moses was an Egyptian . . ." as follows:

Of all the events of early times which later poets, priests and historians undertook to work over, one stood out, the suppression of which was enjoined by the most immediate and best human motives. This was the murder of Moses, the great leader and liberator, which Sellin *discovered* from hints in the writings of the Prophets. Sellin's hypothesis cannot be called fantastic – it is probable enough. Moses, deriving from the school of Akhenaten, employed no methods other than did the king; he commanded, he forced his faith upon the people. The doctrine of Moses may have been even harsher than that of his master. He had no need to retain the sun-god as a support: the school of On had no significance for his alien people. Moses, like Akhenaten, met with the same fate that awaits all enlightened despots. The Jewish people under Moses were just as little able to tolerate such a highly spiritualized [*vergeistigte*] religion and find satisfaction of their needs in what it had to offer as had been the Egyptians of the Eighteenth Dynasty. The same thing happened in both cases: those who had been dominated and kept in want rose and threw off the burden of the religion that had been imposed on them. But while the tame Egyptians waited till fate had removed the sacred figure of their Pharaoh, the savage Semites took fate into their own hands and rid themselves of their tyrant. (23:47, emphasis added)[16]

I suggested earlier that throughout this second essay there is an implicit valorization of Jewish monotheism. This might seem to be belied by the adjectives Freud uses to characterize monotheism: "strict," "rigid," "intolerant," and "exclusive." But in the Freudian lexicon these are not necessarily pejorative expressions. Rather they are indicative of the rigorous "spiritual and intellectual" (*geistig*) demands that monotheism places upon us, demands similar to the rigorous intellectual require-ments of psychoanalysis.

Freud's own praise for the Mosaic teaching, and his pride in the Jewish tradition of the Prophets, can clearly be discerned in a passage that comes near the end of "If Moses was an Egyptian . . ." – a passage that helps us to understand this ellipsis. Even Freud's prose assumes a biblical cadence:

Thereupon there arose from among the midst of the people an unending succession of men who were not linked to Moses in their origin but were enthralled by the great and mighty tradition which had grown up little by little in obscurity: and it was these men, the Prophets, who tirelessly preached the old Mosaic doctrine – that the deity disdained sacrifice and ceremonial and asked only for faith and a life in truth and justice (Ma'at). The efforts of the Prophets had a lasting success; the doctrines with which they re-established the old faith became the permanent content of the Jewish religion. It is honour enough to the Jewish people that they could preserve such a tradition and produce men who gave it a voice – even though the initiative to it came from outside, from a great foreigner. (23:51)[17]

This enlightened Mosaic teaching; this *geistig* teaching that abhors magic, sorcery, and the craving for graven images; this teaching that asks "only for faith and a life in truth and justice" eventually triumphed. This is the tradition that was preached by the Prophets – one that the Jewish people (including Freud the Jew) can honor and be proud of. This is the "great and mighty" tradition with which Freud the "godless Jew" identifies. When we complete our analysis of Part III of *The Man Moses and the Monotheistic Religion*, we will see clearly that this is why Freud "feels that he is in his essential nature a Jew." But already, Freud's understanding of the Mosaic ideal and Jewish monotheism as establishing a tradition that places such a high and rigorous demand on living a life of truth and justice without falling back to any form of idolatry is anticipated in his first two essays.

HISTORICAL INTERLUDE: FROM VIENNA TO LONDON

In the opening paragraph of "If Moses was an Egyptian . . ." Freud uses the metaphor of "a bronze statue with feet of clay," a recurring metaphor that Freud employs with slight variations in his correspondence. I agree with Yerushalmi that the "imposing" bronze statue refers to the third essay, Part III of *The Man Moses and the Monotheistic Religion* (*FM*, 22). But before turning to an examination of this essay, I want to consider the historical circumstances of Freud's preoccupation with the Egyptian origin of Moses and the character of Jewish monotheism. Freud freely discusses the progress of his inquiry in his correspondence during the 1930s. This correspondence provides a rich source for discovering how Freud conceived of his work, why he was motivated to write it, and why he was so reluctant to publish it.

Freud's first two essays were published in *Imago* in 1937 when he was still living in Vienna. In both essays, Freud gives us hints about the consequences he intends to draw from the "fact" that Moses was an Egyptian aristocrat who chose the Jews to be the followers of Akhenaten's monotheism, but he writes as if drawing out these consequences is still work to be done in the future – work which he may never complete. In 1937, Freud was eighty-one years old, he was suffering from a painful and debilitating cancer, and anticipating his own death. In 1937, Freud was still resisting the pleas from his family and friends to escape from Vienna. We know now, however, that already in 1934, Freud "conceived, and for the most part wrote, his ideas on Moses and religion, ideas that were to engross him for the rest of his life."[18] Freud's 1934 manuscript draft contains the central theses that we find in the third essay of *The Man Moses and the Monotheistic Religion* – the very material that he referred to as *future* work to be done in the concluding paragraph of "If Moses was an Egyptian . . ." On 6 November, 1934, three years prior to the publication of the first two essays, Freud wrote to Arnold Zweig, "I need more certainty and I should not like to endanger the final formula of the whole book which I regard as valuable, by founding it on a base of clay."[19] On 16 December, 1934 he wrote again, indicating his hesitancy about publishing his results:

Don't say any more about the Moses book. The fact that this, probably my last creative effort, should have come to grief depresses me enough as it is. Not that I can shake him off. The man and what I wanted to make of him pursue me everywhere. But it would not do; the external dangers and inner misgivings allow of no other solution. I think my memory of recent events is no longer reliable. The fact that I wrote at length to you in an earlier letter about Moses being an Egyptian is not the essential point, though it is the starting point. Nor is it any inner uncertainty of my part, for that is as good as settled, but the fact that I was obliged to construct so imposing a statue upon feet of clay, so that any fool could topple it. (*SFAZ*, 98)

This frank admission supports what we have already discovered in the texts of the first two essays. Despite Freud's reiterated claims about the uncertainty of his historical claims, he was confident that he had correctly guessed and interpreted what happened to Moses in the wilderness. After completing his 1934 draft which he entitled *Der Mann Moses: Ein historischer Roman* (The Man Moses: An Historical Novel), Freud was still searching for evidence to support his historical claims. On 2 May, 1935, he wrote to Arnold Zweig that he had discovered in an account of Tel-el-Amarna the mention of a Prince Thotmes, "of whom nothing further is known." "If I were a millionaire, I would finance the continuation of these excavations. This Thotmes could be my Moses and I would be able to boast that *I had guessed right*" (*SFAZ*, 106, emphasis added).

Despite Freud's anxiety about the paucity of objective evidence to support his historical reconstruction, he was obsessed with his *Moses* study. When the book was finally published in 1939 Freud confesses: "Actually it has been written twice: for the first time a few years ago in Vienna, where I did not think it would be possible to publish it. I determined to give it up; but it tormented me like an unlaid ghost . . ." (23:103). Freud did not want to submit to the public a bronze statue with feet of clay – to expose himself to ridicule. But this is not the main reason for holding back the publication of the "dangerous" third essay. In the first prefatory note to Part III of his book, a preface that was written *before* March 12, 1938 when the Germans marched into Austria, he explicitly states: "So I shall not give this work to the public. But that need not prevent my writing it . . . It may then be preserved in concealment till some day the time arrives when it may venture without danger into the light, or till someone who has reached the same conclusions and opinions can be told: 'there was someone in darker times who thought the same as you!'" (23:56).   Why was Freud so reluctant to publish the third essay of his book, the part that he characterized as "full of content," and "which included what was really open to objection and dangerous – the application [of these findings] to the genesis of monotheism and the view of religion in general . . ." (23:103)? One might think that, in light of what was happening to European Jewry, Freud hesitated to offend his fellow Jews. But this was not what was foremost in his mind. Freud was far more wary of what he believed would be the reaction of the Catholic authorities. In the same prefatory note mentioned above, he wrote the following:

We are living here in a Catholic country under the protection of that Church, uncertain how long that protection will hold out. But as long as it lasts, we naturally hesitate to do anything that would be bound to arouse the Church's hostility. This is not cowardice, but prudence. The new enemy, to whom we want to avoid being of service, is more dangerous than the old one with whom we have already learnt to come to terms. The psycho-analytic researches which we carry on are in any case viewed with suspicious attention by Catholicism. I will not maintain that this is unjustly so. If our work leads us to a conclusion which reduces religion to a neurosis of humanity and explains its enormous power in the same way as a neurotic compulsion in our individual patients, we may be sure of drawing the resentment of our ruling powers down upon us . . . It would probably lead to our being prohibited from practising psycho-analysis. Such violent methods of suppression are, indeed, by no means alien to the Church; the fact is rather that it feels it as an invasion of its privileges if someone else makes use of those methods. But psycho-analysis, which in the course of my long life has gone everywhere, still possesses no home that could be more valuable for it than the city in which it was born and grew up. (23:55)

Whatever judgment we may make about the soundness of Freud's reasoning, his own political assessment of the Catholic Church, and whether prudence was the appropriate response in such a situation, there is little doubt that this is what was uppermost in Freud's mind. Freud expressed the same concern in his correspondence. In a letter to Arnold Zweig dated 9 September, 1934, he writes:

Faced with the new persecutions, one asks oneself again how the Jews have come to be what they are and why they have attracted this undying hatred. I soon discovered the formula: Moses created the Jews. So I gave my book the title: *The Man Moses, a historical novel . . .* The material fits into three sections. The first part is like an interesting novel; the second is laborious and boring; the third is full of content and makes exacting reading. The whole enterprise broke down on this third section, for it involved a theory of religion – certainly nothing new for me after *Totem and Taboo*, but something new and fundamental for the uninitiated. It is the thought of these uninitiated readers that makes me hold over the finished work. For we live here in an atmosphere of Catholic orthodoxy. They say that the politics of our country are determined by one Pater Schmidt . . . He is a confidant of the Pope, and unfortunately he himself is an ethnologist and a student of comparative religion, whose books make no secret of his abhorrence of analysis and especially of my totem theory . . . Now, any publication of mine will be sure to attract a certain amount of attention, which will not escape the notice of this inimical priest. Thus we might be risking a ban on psychoanalysis in Vienna and the suspension of all our publications here. If this danger involved me alone, I would be but little concerned, but to deprive all our members in Vienna of their livelihood is too great a responsibility. (*SFAZ,* 91 – 2)[20]

And in his letter to Lou Andreas-Salomé (1 June, 1935) in which he gives a succinct account of his main theses concerning Moses and monotheism, he concludes:

And now you see, Lou, this formula, which holds so great a fascination for me, cannot be publicly expressed in Austria today, without bringing down upon us a state prohibition of analysis on the part of the ruling Catholic authority. And it is only this Catholicism which protects us from the Nazis. And furthermore the historical foundations of the Moses story are not solid enough to serve as a basis for these invaluable conclusions of mine. And so I remain silent. It suffices me that I myself can believe in the solution of the problem. *It has pursued me throughout the whole of my life.* (*SFLA*, 205; Appendix, p. 118, emphasis added)[21]

In retrospect, we can see just how politically naive Freud was in understanding what was really going on in Germany and Austria, but there is still a further question that we need to ask. Why was Freud so obsessed with his Moses study? What precisely was "the problem" that Freud thought he had now solved – the problem that had pursued him "throughout the whole of [his] life"? This does not refer to the hypotheses that Moses was an Egyptian, that he "created the Jews," and was murdered by the Jews. For there is no evidence that Freud even formulated these hypotheses prior to the 1930s, although he did have a life long fascination with Moses.[22] The problem that Freud thought that he had now solved was to give an account of the essential character of the Jewish people and their tradition inspired by Moses' monotheistic ideals. He also believed that this would help to explain why the Jews had been the object of such virulent anti-Semitism and "undying hatred" throughout their long history. But we will only fully understand the meaning of Freud's solution (one which answers the question raised in the preface to the Hebrew edition of *Totem and Taboo*), when we analyze Part III of *The Man Moses and the Monotheistic Religion*.

In June, 1938 – after some harrowing experiences in which the Gestapo searched his house and his daughter Anna had been arrested (but released) – Freud was finally allowed to leave Vienna and travel to London. Within a month after his arrival he wrote a second prefatory note for Part III of his *Moses* book. He was now determined to publish the entire book as soon as possible. This is how he explained his decision.

PREFATORY NOTE II
([LONDON], JUNE, 1938)

The quite special difficulties which have weighed on me during my composition of this study relating to the figure of Moses – internal doubts as well as external obstacles – have resulted in this third and concluding essay being introduced by two different prefaces, which contradict each other and indeed cancel each other out. For in the short space of time between the two there has been a fundamental change in the author's circumstances. At the earlier date I was living under the protection of the Catholic Church, and was afraid that the publication of my work would result in the loss of that protection and would conjure up a prohibition upon the work of the adherents and students of psycho-analysis in Austria. Then, suddenly, came the German invasion and Catholicism proved, to use the words of the Bible, 'a broken reed'. In the certainty that I should now be persecuted not only for my line of thought but also for my 'race' – accompanied by many of my friends, I left the city which, from my early childhood, had been my home for seventy-eight years.

I met with the friendliest reception in lovely, free, magnanimous England. Here I now live, a welcome guest; I can breathe a sigh of relief now that the weight has been taken off me and that I am once more able to speak and write – I had almost said 'and think' – as I wish or as I must. I venture to bring the last portion of my work before the public. (23:57)

Although there were those who urged Freud to suppress the publication of his book, or at least to modify some of his claims, Freud resisted these suggestions. The entire book was finally published in 1939 in Amsterdam. In the same year, an English translation by Katherine Jones (the wife of Ernest Jones) also appeared. It was the last book Freud published (although not the last manuscript that he wrote). Freud died on September 23, 1939.

CHAPTER 2

Tradition, trauma, and the return of the repressed

"THE MOST IMPORTANT PART OF THE STORY"

The stylistic structure of the final version of *The Man Moses and the Monotheistic Religion* is extremely awkward and confusing. Freud, who took special pride in his style, deplored its "inartistic quality" but found himself "unable to wipe out the traces of the history of the work's origin, which was in any case unusual" (23:103). The first two parts consist of unrevised versions of the two essays that he had previously published in *Imago*. The third essay (which is almost twice as long as the first two essays together) begins with the two "contradictory" prefaces – the first written before the *Anschluss* in March 1938, and the second preface written in England shortly after his arrival in June 1938. The main body of this third essay is itself divided into two parts. The first part consists of five sections which have the following titles: (A) The Historical Premiss; (B) The Latency Period and Tradition; (C) The Analogy; (D) Application; (E) Difficulties. Part II begins with a section entitled "Summary and Recapitulation," which reads like still another (a third) preface. This is then followed by nine sections: (A) The People of Israel; (B) The Great Man; (C) The Advance in Intellectuality; (D) Renunciation of Instinct; (E) What is True in Religion; (F) The Return of the Repressed; (G) Historical Truth; (H) The Historical Development.[1]

This schematic outline indicates the variety of topics that Freud discusses, and the way in which Freud shuttles between historical and psychoanalytic themes. Is there any unity here? Or if not unity, can we detect some unifying threads running through Freud's discussion of these rich and variegated topics? I believe that we can. In order to clarify what I mean, I want to return to where Freud left off (and left us) at the end of the first two essays which he had published in *Imago* in 1937.

Presumably, Freud had established that Moses was an Egyptian aristocrat or priest who was a follower of the monotheistic religion of

[handwritten margin note: What is motivating Freud given the historical climate of the time Vienna 1930's]

Akhenaten. Because there was no possibility of continuing this religion in Egypt after the death of Akhenaten, Moses chose the "backward" Semites who were residing in Egypt to become the followers of this new monotheism. These Semites were then circumcised (which Freud claims was an established Egyptian practice) so that they would not feel inferior to the Egyptians. And because the Egyptians had returned to their traditional polytheism, Moses led the Jews out of Egypt into the wilderness in order to found a new kingdom. But the Jews soon found that the strict monotheistic religion that Moses forced upon them was too severe and demanding. They rebelled and murdered their leader, Moses. Initially, they returned to their polytheistic religion – the religion that they followed before the "foreigner" Moses led them out of Egypt. Sometime later, at a locality known as Kadesh, the Egyptian Semites joined with other tribes who worshipped the demon volcanic god, Yahweh. There arose a new priest who was not an Egyptian but a Midianite, but who had the same name as the Egyptian Moses. There was a blending of the two religions – a blending of the original Egyptian monotheism and the religion of the Midianites who worshipped the volcanic god, Yahweh.

Now let us suppose that all these events (and the other historical details that Freud relates) actually took place just as Freud claims. Would accepting this "historical" account enable us to draw any conclusions about the character of the Jewish people *today*? Would it explain the "special character of the Jewish people, a character which is probably what has made their survival to the present day possible" (23:123)? The answer – even on the most generous understanding of what Freud has shown *thus* far – must be a definitive "No"! What do these "historical" events which presumably occurred in the fourteenth century BCE have to do with the later history of the Jewish people? Thus far, nothing in Freud's historical exposition explains the relation of these events to what happened subsequently in Jewish history or to what has shaped the Jewish tradition. But it is the linkage between these "historical" events and their psychoanalytic interpretation that is the heart of Freud's argument – an argument that is elaborated only in the third and concluding part of *The Man Moses and the Monotheistic Religion*.

If we carefully read what Freud says in his first two essays, it becomes clear that this connection is precisely what Freud has had in mind. After summarizing his "concise formula" about the dualities in Jewish history in the concluding paragraph of "If Moses was an Egyptian . . .," Freud veils his crucial point in what seems to be an innocuous remark:

"Beyond this there would be a very great deal to discuss, to explain and
to assert. Only thus would an interest in our purely historical study find
its true justification" (23:52). This is immediately followed by what is, in
effect, a précis of the main issues that he addresses in his third essay
"Moses, His People and Monotheist Religion," and which he had
already elaborated in his 1934 draft! Let me return to a passage that I
have already quoted but which now takes on a new and vital significance.

What the real nature of a tradition resides in, and what its special power rests
on, how impossible it is to dispute the personal influence upon world-history of
individual great men, what sacrilege one commits against the splendid diversity
of human life if one recognizes only those motives which arise from material
needs, from what sources some ideas (and particularly religious ones) derive
their power to subject both men and peoples to their yoke – to study all this in
the special case of Jewish history would be an alluring task. To continue my
work on such lines as these would be to find a link with the statements I put
forward twenty-five years ago in *Totem and Taboo* [1912–1913]. But I no longer
feel that I have the strength to do so. (23:52–3)

This passage not only outlines the anticipated third essay, it is, in effect,
a summary statement of the conclusions he had already reached in his
1934 draft (and which he communicated to Lou Andreas-Salomé in his
letter dated 1 June, 1935). It also provides a key for "the most important
part of the whole story." For the thread that runs through Part III of *The
Man Moses and the Monotheistic Religion* is "the real nature" and "special
power" of *tradition*. Yerushalmi, Derrida, and Assmann are among the
very few readers of Freud's *Moses* to have made this point. Yerushalmi
forcefully tells us:

What readers of *Moses and Monotheism* have generally failed to recognize –
perhaps because they have been too preoccupied with its more sensational
aspects of Moses the Egyptian and his murder by the Jews – is that the *true axis of
the book, especially of the all-important part III, is the problem of tradition, not merely its
origins, but above all its dynamics.* (*FM*, 29, emphasis added)

What does Freud mean by tradition? What are the dynamics of tradition? How is one to account for the power of religious tradition – and in
particular, the Jewish tradition? And how is tradition related to what
Freud calls "historical truth"? The answers to these questions "are the
most important part of the whole story." Freud's answers are complex
and subtle. They take us to the very core of psychoanalysis, and will
require exploring a number of byways before we can fully appreciate

how *The Man Moses and the Monotheistic Religion* answers the question that
Freud so cryptically raised in the preface to the Hebrew edition of *Totem
and Taboo*.

TRADITION: THE PROBLEM OF THE "GAP"

In order to prepare the way for answering these questions, let me start
with a sketch of Freud's account of what happened to the Jewish people
after the traumatic event of the murder of Moses in the wilderness.

After the slaying of Moses, the Egyptian Semites reverted to a more
primitive idolatry and polytheism. This parallels what had already
happened in Egypt after the death of Akhenaten when the Egyptian
priests of Amun proved victorious and sought (unsuccessfully) to obliterate all traces of the monotheistic Aten religion. The major difference is
that whereas the Egyptian priests waited until the death of Akhenaten,
the Egyptian Semites in the wilderness did not wait until Moses died;
they murdered him. The immediate descendants of the Semitic tribe
that Moses led out of Egypt "had good motives for repressing the
memory of the fate with which their leader and lawgiver had met"
(23:68). "[T]here was a long period after the defection from the religion
of Moses during which no sign was to be detected of the monotheist
idea, of the contempt for ceremonial or of the great emphasis on ethics"
(23:68). Even the worship of the new god Yahweh was originally not a
form of monotheism. For Yahweh was only one god among the gods of
other peoples. The trauma of the murder of the imposing father-figure
Moses was repressed and virtually all traces of this murder were obliterated. But the Jews did not remain followers of the two religions that
were artificially blended at Kadesh. Like "the return of the repressed" –
after a long gap – monotheism ultimately proved victorious. It is this
"gap" that fascinates Freud, and presents a special problem for him. To
signal the importance of this problem, Freud (three times) refers to it as
remarkable and strange (*merkwürdig*).

The remarkable fact [*Die merkwürdige Tatsache*] with which we are here confronted is, however, that these traditions, instead of becoming weaker with
time, became more and more powerful in the course of centuries, forced their
way into the later official accounts and finally showed themselves strong
enough to have a decisive influence on the thoughts and actions of the people.
(23:69)

The fact is so remarkable [*Diese Tatsache ist so merkwürdig*] that we feel justified in
looking at it once again. Our problem is comprised in it. The Jewish people had

abandoned the Aten religion brought to them by Moses and had turned to the worship of another god who differed little from the Baalim of the neighbouring peoples. All the tendentious efforts of later times failed to disguise this shameful fact. But the Mosaic religion had not vanished without leaving a trace; some sort of memory of it had kept alive – a possibly obscured and distorted tradition. And it was this tradition of a great past which continued to operate (from the background, as it were), which gradually acquired more and more power over people's minds and which in the end succeeded in changing the god Yahweh into the Mosaic god and in re-awakening into life the religion of Moses that had been introduced and then abandoned long centuries before. (23:69–70)

Even earlier in his text, Freud says:

The remarkable thing [*Merkwürdige*], however, is that that ["the final end of the Moses episode in the history of the Jewish people"] was not the case – that the most powerful effects of the people's experience were to come to light only later and to force their way into reality in the course of many centuries. (23:62)

I will return to this "gap" and the problem that it presents for Freud shortly, but I want to continue Freud's overall narrative of what happened to the Jewish people. It was the monotheism of Moses with its harsh disdain for all forms of idolatry, and its emphasis on leading an ethical life of truth and justice that eventually came to prevail.

Freud calls this development "*Der Fortschritt in der Geistigkeit*" – a phrase that is almost impossible to translate. Strachey translates this phrase as "The Advance in Intellectuality" and Katherine Jones translates it as "The Progress in Spirituality." One can well understand why Strachey has resorted to translating *Geistigkeit* with the cumbersome phrase "intellectuality and spirituality." In English (although not in its Latin etymology), "intellectuality" or "intellectual" fails to convey the power and dynamic quality of the German "*Geist.*" In some of its English usages, "spirituality" not only lacks the intellectual and rational significance of the German "*Geist,*" but is even sometimes used in contrast to what is truly "intellectual." Freud, a master of the German language and the German cultural tradition, was fully aware of the significant resonances of "*Geist*" (and its cognates). In selecting the expression "*Geistigkeit*" Freud was not only exhibiting his acute linguistic sensitivity, but also indicating what he takes to be the most important and substantive achievement of the tradition initiated by Mosaic monotheism in shaping the character of the Jewish people.

Freud gives his own linguistic account of the "origin" of *Geist.*

Human beings found themselves obliged in general to recognise 'intellectual' [*geistige*] forces – forces, that is, which cannot be grasped by the senses (particularly by the sight) but which none the less produce undoubted and indeed extremely powerful effects. If we may rely upon the evidence of language, it was movement of the air that provided the prototype of intellectuality [*Geistigkeit*], for intellect [*Geist*] derives its name from a breath of wind – '*animus*', '*spiritus*', and the Hebrew '*ruach* (breath)'. This too led to the discovery of the mind [*Seele* (soul)] as that of the intellectual [*geistigen*] principle in individual human beings. (23:114)[2]

This advance deeply marked the character of the Jewish people; it brought about "lasting psychical results in [the Jewish] people" (23:111). The "return of the repressed" – the return of the religion of the Egyptian Moses – contributed to the Jews' "enhancement of their self-esteem owing to their consciousness of having been chosen" (23:112).

Yerushalmi astutely observes that Lou Andreas-Salomé was one of the first (and very few) to have "intuitively grasped an essential aspect of *Moses and Monotheism* that has largely escaped Freud's commentators" (*FM*, 78). In 1935 when Freud sent her a summary of his ideas, she "responded with an excitement that matched his own" (*FM*, 78).

[W]hat particularly fascinated *me* in your present view of things is a specific characteristic of the 'return of the repressed', namely, the way in which noble and precious elements return despite long intermixture with every conceivable kind of material . . .
    Hitherto we have usually understood the term 'return of the repressed' in the context of neurotic processes: all kinds of material which had been wrongly repressed afflicted the neurotic mysteriously with phantoms out of the past . . . which he felt bound to ward off. But in this case we are presented with examples of the survival of the most triumphantly vital elements of the past as the truest possession in the present, despite all the destructive elements and counterforces they have endured. (*SFLA*, 206-7)

We can see how insightful Lou Andreas-Salomé had been when we compare what she says with what Freud wrote in his section "*Der Fortschritt in der Geistigkeit*." The religion of Moses "also brought the Jews a far grander conception of God, or, as we might put it more modestly, the conception of a grander God. Anyone who believed in this God had some kind of share in his greatness, might feel exalted himself" (23:112). Freud describes the significance of the Mosaic prohibition against making images of God as follows:

Among the precepts of the Moses religion there is one that is of greater importance than appears to begin with. This is the prohibition against making an image of God – the compulsion to worship a God whom one cannot see. In

[handwritten: THE EGYPTIAN PHAROAH DID NOT GO THIS FAR — A TRANSCENDENT GOD — OVERRIDES A PAN-THEISM]

this, I suspect, Moses was outdoing the strictness of the Aten religion. Perhaps he merely wanted to be consistent; his God would in that case have neither a name nor a countenance.) Perhaps it was a fresh measure against magical abuses. But if this prohibition were accepted, it must have a profound effect. For it meant that a sensory perception was given second place to what may be called an abstract idea – a triumph of intellectuality [*Geistigkeit*] over sensuality [*Sinnlichkeit*] or, strictly speaking, an instinctual renunciation, with all its necessary psychological consequences. (23:112–13)

[handwritten: ISSUE OF GAZE/VOICE]

Strachey translates the German phrase "*einen Triumph der Geistigkeit über die Sinnlichkeit*" as "a triumph of intellectuality over sensuality" whereas Katherine Jones translates it as "a triumph of spirituality over the senses." I think that Jones's translation is more accurate because "*Sinnlichkeit*" is the standard German term for referring to the senses and to what can be known by sensory perception. (This is the standard term used to refer to the senses in the tradition of German Idealism.) The important contrast that Freud draws is between the "lower" form of knowledge that is grasped by the senses and a "higher" form of abstract intellectual (spiritual) knowledge. This triumph over sensory perception requires "an instinctual renunciation, with its necessary psychological consequences." When the Jews killed Moses, they were rebelling against the rigorous *geistige* demands of a strict monotheism that prohibited sensuous images; a monotheism that required instinctual renunciation. But in the course of Jewish history, the *Geistigkeit* demanded by Mosaic monotheism has been victorious in defining Judaism.

[handwritten right margin: HENO-THEISM SACRIFICE FROM VISUAL REP. AVAILABLE TO SENSES (ZEUS) EACH PERSON CAN DEV. A MORE PERSONAL RELATION-SHIP W/ THE GOD NOW ALL PEOPLE MUST SHARE THIS UNFORSEEN GOD SACRIFICE OF INSTINCTUAL GRATIFICA-TION]

What Freud says in the above passage not only echoes, but virtually repeats much of what Kant declares in his characterization of the sublime in his *Critique of Judgment*. Kant also emphasizes the supremacy of intellectuality over sensibility, and he relates this directly to the Jewish prohibition of graven images.

Hence the sublime must always have reference to our way of *thinking*, i.e., to maxims directed to providing the intellectual [side in us] and our rational ideas with supremacy and sensibility.

We need not worry that the feeling of the sublime will lose [something] if it is exhibited in such an abstract way as this, which is wholly negative as regards the sensible. For though the imagination finds nothing beyond the sensible that could support it, this very removal of its barriers also makes it feel unbounded, so that its separation [from the sensible] is an exhibition of the infinite; and though an exhibition of the infinite can as such never be more than merely negative, it still expands the soul. Perhaps the most sublime passage in the Jewish Law is the commandment: Thou shalt not make unto thee any graven image, or any likeness of any thing that is in heaven or on earth, or under the

[handwritten: TEMPLE IS REPLACED BY THE BOOK — DIFFERENT FORMS OF WORSHIP THROUGH RITUAL AND STUDY]

earth, etc. This commandment alone can explain the enthusiasm that the Jewish people in its civilized era felt for its religion when it compared itself with other peoples . . .

Kant was not alone in the eighteenth century in emphasizing the sublimity of this conception of God. Schiller, in his famous essay *Die Sendung Moses* (The Legation of Moses) – an essay which Freud probably read in his youth – also stresses the sublimity of this conception of God: "Nothing is more sublime than the simple grandeur with which the sages spoke of the creator. In order to distinguish him in a truly defining form, they refrained from giving him a name at all." Schiller's essay appeared in the same year as the first edition of the *Critique of Judgment* (1790).[3]

Freud continues to spell out the consequences of this *Fortschritt in der Geistigkeit* for the Jewish people.

All such advances in intellectuality have as their consequence that the individual's self-esteem is increased, that he is made proud – so that he feels superior to other people who have remained under the spell of sensuality. Moses, as we know, conveyed to the Jews an exalted sense of being a chosen people. The dematerialization of God brought a fresh and valuable contribution to their secret treasure. The Jews retained their inclination to intellectual interests. The nation's political misfortune taught it to value at its true worth the one possession that remained to it – its literature. Immediately after the destruction of the Temple in Jerusalem by Titus, the Rabbi Jochanan ben Zakkai asked permission to open the first Torah school at Jabneh. From that time on, the Holy Writ and intellectual concern with it were what held the scattered people together. (23: 115)

In 1938, a delegation visited Freud in London to renew his interest in the Yivo Institute (the Institute for Yiddish studies which was founded in Vilna in 1925). After this visit Freud wrote the following passage which is even more emphatic in stressing the significance of (and Freud's identification with) Rabbi Jochanan ben Zakkai.

We, Jews, have always cherished spiritual values. Ideas have held us together and by virtue of them we have survived to this day. One of the most significant events in our history to me was Rabbi Yohanan ben Zakkai's plea to the conqueror, immediately after the destruction of the Temple, for permission to establish the first academy of Jewish learning in Yavneh. Once again our people are facing difficult times. They call for a mustering of all our strength to preserve unharmed our culture and learning.[4]

Richard L. Rubenstein makes an extremely perceptive comment about Freud's identification with Rabbi ben Zakkai.

THEOLOGIAN

Freud directly identified himself with the one rabbi who, in Jewish tradition, was regarded as most responsible for the continuation of the traditions of the Torah in the face of Roman oppression. He saw himself as proceeding to London to found a new Jabneh where the new Torah would survive and grow. Anyone who has had rabbinic training has had the story of Rabbi Johanan ben Zakkai engraved on his psyche a thousand times. It is the paradigmatic story of the survival of Judaism under conditions of defeat.[5]

Freud, in the passages we have cited, is no longer the disinterested psychoanalyst seeking to understand the origin and nature of Jewish monotheism, but speaking in his own voice as a passionate "godless *Jew*," taking pride in the spiritual and intellectual power of his *own* tradition. These passages illuminate why Freud proudly affirms himself as a member of the Jewish people – the inheritor of an intellectual, ethical, and spiritual tradition inspired by "the great man" Moses.

We can also begin to understand why "the true axis of the book . . . is the problem of tradition, not merely its origins, but above all its dynamics" (*FM*, 29). If it is true that there has been this powerful "return of the repressed," this "return" of the grandeur of the Jewish monotheistic religion in the course of a developing Jewish tradition, we need an account of the dynamics of this process. It is here that psychoanalysis can make its most distinctive contribution. In order to understand how psychoanalysis sheds light on how the Mosaic religion – after a long period of latency – came to dominate the thinking and everyday lives of the Jewish people, we must turn our attention to the investigation of the psychological sources and prehistory of religion itself. Freud has already provided us with the essential clue about the direction of his thinking in "If Moses was an Egyptian . . . " In the penultimate sentence of this essay, he writes: "To continue my work on such lines as these would be to find a link with the statements I put forward twenty-five years ago in *Totem and Taboo*" (23:53).[6]

FROM TOTEMISM TO MONOTHEISM

Freud never gave up the views that he had advanced in *Totem and Taboo*, even though in the intervening twenty-five years he had been severely criticized about the use that he made of anthropological and ethnographic evidence.[7] Despite these objections, Freud did not waver in his conviction that he had discovered the psychological origins of religion and morality in totemistic practices. But what precisely is the link between *Totem and Taboo* and *The Man Moses and the Monotheistic Religion*?

"ARCHIVE FEVER" - DERRIDA

In the third part of his *Moses* book, after reviewing "the formula that [Freud had] laid down for the development of a neurosis" in an individual – "[e]arly trauma – defence – latency – outbreak of neurotic illness – partial return of the repressed," he invites his readers "to take the step of supposing that something occurred in the life of the human species similar to what occurs in the life of individuals" (23:80). Freud then gives a brief summary of *Totem and Taboo* – in particular, the story of how primitive men lived in small hordes dominated by a strong male – a powerful father. The sons who fear being killed or castrated by the father rise up against him, murder him, and devour him. Convinced that the analogy between "primitive men" and "the primitives of the present day" – our children – warrants attributing the emotional attitudes that we discover in children to these "primitive hordes," Freud writes: "We suppose, that is, that they not only hated and feared their father but also honoured him as a model, and that each of them wished to take his place in reality. We can, if so, understand the cannibalistic act as an attempt to ensure identification with him by incorporating a piece of him" (23:82).

The first form of a social organization [of the brothers] came about with a *renunciation of instinct*, a recognition of mutual *obligations*, the introduction of definite *institutions*, pronounced inviolable (holy) – that is to say, the beginnings of morality and justice. Each individual renounced his ideal of acquiring his father's position for himself and of possessing his mother and sisters. Thus the *taboo on incest* and the injunction to *exogamy* came about . . . A powerful animal – at first, perhaps, always one that was feared as well – was chosen as a substitute for the father. (23:82)

The psychological ambivalence of the brothers toward their father is retained in the ambivalence to the totem animal which is at once feared and honored. Drawing upon the research of Robertson Smith, Freud argues that the devouring of the father by the cannibalistic sons is the basis for totemic festivals in which the totemic animal – like the primal father – is killed and devoured.

I am skipping over an important stage in this narrative just as Freud does – the role of matriarchy in the sequence of religions. Freud describes the move away from totemism as follows:

The first step away from totemism was the humanizing of the being who was worshipped. In place of the animals, human gods appear, whose derivation from the totem is not concealed. The god is still represented either in the form of an animal or at least with an animal's face, or the totem becomes the god's favourite companion, inseparable from him, or legend tells us that the god slew this precise animal, which was after all only a preliminary stage of himself. At a point in this evolution which is not easily determined great mother-goddesses appeared, probably even before the male gods, and afterwards persisted for a long time beside them. (23:83)

In his *Moses* book, Freud does not explore this religious stage when the mother-goddesses appeared. He does not explore in depth the role of matriarchy in the history of religion. Indeed, he no sooner opens up this fascinating topic than he closes it by pointing out that a great social revolution occurred in which "[m]atriarchy was succeeded by the re-establishment of a patriarchal order" (23:83). It is the patriarchal development in religion that is Freud's dominant concern. The primary accent in Freud's narrative of the development of religion is the Oedipal confrontation of sons and fathers.

It should also be noted that except for a casual reference to Akhenaten's mother, Freud completely neglects the role of powerful women in Akhenaten's life – especially his mother, Queen Tiye; his primary wife, Nefertiti; and his six daughters. Freud, in passing, comments: "And he [Akhenaten], whose greatness as the founder of a religion is unequivocally established, may perhaps have been following hints which had reached him – from near or distant parts of Asia – through the medium of his mother or by other paths" (23:110). As Strachey points out "The theory held at one time, that Akhenaten's mother, Queen Tiye, was of foreign origin, had been abandoned in view of the discovery of her parents' tomb at Thebes" (23:110). Some Egyptologists believe that it was primarily Queen Tiye who was responsible for the religious reform introduced during Akhenaten's reign – a view that was also advanced by Karl Abraham.[8]

I am further condensing Freud's own condensation of the conclusions in *Totem and Taboo* because I want to highlight those features of this "story" of the primitive horde that are relevant to his *Moses* study. The key point is that totemism is "the first form in which religion was manifested in human history" and this first form of religion was already linked "with social regulations and moral obligations" (23:83).

To the religiously-based prohibition against killing the totem was now added the socially-based prohibition against fratricide. It was not until long afterwards that the prohibition ceased to be limited to members of the clan and assumed the simple form: 'Thou shalt do no murder.' The patriarchal horde was replaced in the first instance by the fraternal clan, whose existence was assured by the blood tie. Society was now based on complicity in the common crime;

religion was based on the sense of guilt and remorse attaching to it; while morality was based partly on the exigencies of this society and partly on the penance demanded by the sense of guilt. (13:146)

But if this totemism is the first form in which religion arises in human history, how does religion develop? Freud provides a sketchy outline of this development. What is especially fascinating and telling is the way in which Freud intermingles descriptive and evaluative categories in characterizing this development – a development that involves both progress and regression. Thus he tells us: "The first step away from totemism was the *humanizing* [*Vermenschlichung*] of the being who was worshipped" (23:83, emphasis added). At some point in this evolution great "mother-goddesses appeared," but "[m]atriarchy was succeeded by the re-establishment of a patriarchal order." Nevertheless the new fathers "never achieved the omnipotence of the primal father." This then was the beginning of polytheism. It is the next stage in this scheme of the evolution of religion that brings us to the origins of monotheism – the return of a single "father-god of unlimited dominion" (23:84). Freud expands his story to include the "origin" of Christianity out of Jewish monotheism. I want to call attention to the *evaluative* dimension of his account – for it contributes to our deeper appreciation of Freud's own identification with the Jewish tradition. He writes:

In some respects the new religion [Christianity] meant a cultural regression as compared with the older, Jewish one, as regularly happens when a new mass of people, of a lower level, break their way in or are given admission. The Christian religion did not maintain the high level in things of the mind to which Judaism had soared. It was no longer strictly monotheist, it took over numerous symbolic rituals from surrounding peoples, it re-established the great mother-goddess and found room to introduce many of the divine figures of polytheism only lightly veiled, though in subordinate positions. Above all, it did not, like the Aten religion and the Mosaic one which followed it, exclude the entry of superstitious, magical and mystical elements, which were to prove a severe inhibition upon the intellectual development of the next two thousand years.

The triumph of Christianity was a fresh victory for the priests of Amun over Akhenaten's god after an interval of fifteen hundred years and on a wider stage. (23:88)

Freud begins to sound like the biblical Prophets that he so admired – warning us about the dangers of idolatry and the falling away from a "strict monotheism." He sternly reminds us of the heights to which Judaism has soared, and admonishes us against falling back into "superstitious, magical and mystical elements." There is another biblical (and rabbinic) analogy here. The threat of idolatry – whether the victory of the priests of Amun or the worship of the golden calf is not something that happened long ago – it is a constant threat that *repeats* itself (just as the Prophets have declared). And yet, Freud's pronouncements are never quite unambiguous, and never quite without an ironic twist. For the sentence that follows immediately after the passage I have just quoted declares: "And yet in the history of religion – that is, as regards the return of the repressed – Christianity was an advance and from that time on the Jewish religion was to some extent a fossil" (23:88). This is a shocking remark. It has been seized upon by those who are all too ready to think that Freud is adopting a Christian point of view. I will return to the meaning of this claim when I consider Freud's reflections on Saul (Paul) and Christian anti-Semitism.

Still, we want to know what is the point of narrating this history of religions from a psychoanalytic perspective. What is the link between the totemism of the primitive horde and the monotheism of Moses? How does this help us to understand the character, power and dynamics of a religious tradition? Freud indicates the rationale for introducing this material from *Totem and Taboo* into his *Moses* book when he writes:

> If our account of primaeval history is accepted as on the whole worthy of belief, two sorts of elements will be recognized in religious doctrines and rituals: on the one hand fixations to the ancient history of the family and survivals of it, and on the other hand revivals of the past and returns, after long intervals, of what has been forgotten. It is this last portion which, hitherto overlooked and therefore not understood, is to be demonstrated here in at least one impressive instance. It is worth specially stressing the fact that each portion which returns from oblivion asserts itself with peculiar force, exercises an incomparably powerful influence on people in the mass, and raises an irresistible claim to truth against which logical objections remain powerless: a kind of '*credo quia absurdum*'. This remarkable feature can only be understood on the pattern of the delusions of psychotics. We have long understood that a portion of forgotten truth lies hidden in delusional ideas, that when this returns it has to put up with distortions and misunderstandings, and that the compulsive conviction which attaches to the delusion arises from this core of truth and spreads out on to the errors that wrap it round. We must grant an ingredient such as this of what may be called *historical* truth to the dogmas of religion as well, which, it is true, bear the character of psychotic symptoms but which, as group phenomena, escape the curse of isolation. (23:84–5)

We must be careful not to misinterpret what Freud is saying here. It is tempting to think that Freud, despite his claims to the contrary, is giving a reductive account of religion; that he is brutally and simplistically reducing religion to being a matter of "psychotic symptoms," and thereby denigrating the significance of it. Although this is a common way of reading Freud, it does the greatest violence to what he is trying to show us. I have already cited some of the passages in which Freud explicitly states that this is not his intention, and acknowledges that there can be no simple account of the origins and dynamics of religion. Freud acknowledges that his starting point in dealing with religion is what he has learned as a psychoanalyst from the study of individual neurotics, and more generally, from the psychological development of individuals. He is fully aware that it requires an imaginative leap to apply these insights to group phenomena such as the religious life of a people – and that such a leap involves "difficulties." He seeks to explain and to justify the analogy that he is drawing.

This brings us back to the remarkable fact [*Die merkwürdige Tatsache*] that I mentioned earlier – viz., that although the Jewish people initially abandoned monotheism after they murdered Moses, the Mosaic religion did not disappear without a trace. On the contrary, after a long period (centuries) of latency, it eventually gathered more and more power over people's minds and had a powerful effect in shaping the character of the Jewish people. Consider how Freud introduces the section of his third essay entitled "Application":

Early trauma – defence – latency – outbreak of neurotic illness – partial return of the repressed. Such is the formula which we have laid down for the development of a neurosis. The reader is now invited to take the step of supposing that something occurred in the life of the human species similar to what occurs in the life of individuals: of supposing, that is, that here too events occurred of a sexually aggressive nature, which left behind them permanent consequences but were for the most part fended off and forgotten, and which after a long latency came into effect and created phenomena similar to symptoms in their structure and purpose. (23:80)

This formula for the stages of individual neurosis provides the schema for Freud's narrative of the origin and development of totemic religion. Furthermore, this same formulaic pattern is repeated in the history of the Jewish religion. The traumatic event of the murder of Moses is repressed and forgotten. After a long period of latency, there is a "return of the repressed." But the murder of the primal father and the murder of Moses are closely related. The murder of the father is *repeated*.

Fate had brought the great deed and misdeed of primaeval days, the killing of the father, closer to the Jewish people by causing them to repeat it on the person of Moses, an outstanding father-figure. It was a case of 'acting out' instead of remembering . . . (23:88–9)[9]

Psychically, this repetition, this "acting out"[10] is extremely important because it enables us (from a psychoanalytic perspective) to explain the force of the return of the repressed after a period of latency. Consequently "[t]he killing of Moses by his Jewish people . . . thus becomes an indispensable part of our construction, an important link between the forgotten event of primaeval times and its later emergence in the form of the monotheist religions" (23:89).

We learn from psychoanalysis, so Freud argues, that the effects of trauma are of two kinds, positive and negative. Both of these effects have analogies in the development of religion.

The former [positive effects] are attempts to bring the trauma into operation once again – that is, to remember the forgotten experience or, better still, to make it real, to experience a repetition of it anew, or, even if it was only an early emotional relationship, to revive it in an analogous relationship with someone else. We summarize these efforts under the name of 'fixations' to the trauma and as a 'compulsion to repeat'. (23:75)
The negative reactions follow the opposite aim: that nothing of the forgotten traumas shall be remembered and nothing repeated. We can summarize them as 'defensive reactions'. (23:76)

Both of these effects of trauma make the most powerful contributions to the stamping of character in the individual. Insofar as religious phenomena are themselves based upon traumas, these traumatic effects stamp the character of the people who are followers of the religion.

There is another reason why the psychoanalytic concept of latency is so important for Freud's overall argument about the "gap" in the re-assertion of the Mosaic tradition. Freud introduces his discussion of "The Latency Period and Tradition" by illustrating the role of latency in the genesis of "traumatic neurosis."

It may happen that someone gets away, apparently unharmed, from the spot where he has suffered a shocking accident, for instance a train collision. In the course of the following weeks, however, he develops a series of grave psychical and motor symptoms, which can be ascribed only to his shock or whatever else happened at the time of the accident. He has developed a "traumatic neurosis." This appears quite incomprehensible and is therefore a novel fact. The time that elapsed between the accident and the first appearance of the symptoms is called the "incubation period," a transparent allusion to the pathology of infectious disease. As an afterthought we observe that, in spite of the fundamental difference in the two cases – the problem of the traumatic neurosis and that of Jewish monotheism – there is a correspondence in one point. It is the feature which one might term *latency*. There are the best grounds for thinking that in the history of the Jewish religion there is a long period, after the breaking away from the Moses religion, during which no trace is to be found of the monotheistic idea, the condemnation of ceremonial, and the emphasis on the ethical side. Thus we are prepared for the possibility that the solution of our problem is to be sought in a special psychological situation.[11]

Although Freud cautions the reader that this example may seem to have little in common to "our problem," it is actually quite pivotal. The analogy helps us to understand the belatedness of the return of the repressed and the power of the resurgence of the Mosaic religion. It enables us to understand that the trauma experienced by the Jewish people did not arise at the time of the murder of Moses. (Just as the trauma experienced by an individual does not arise at the time of the "shocking accident.") An individual may well have a conscious memory of what happened after an accident. But this conscious memory is not the trauma. Strictly speaking, the genesis of a trauma is not to be identified with an event that arises at a specific moment in time. The temporality of latency and trauma is extremely complex. Cathy Caruth (who cites the above passage) in her "Introduction" to *Trauma: Explorations in Memory* perceptively remarks:

In the term "latency," the period during which the effects of the experience are not apparent, Freud seems to describe the trauma as the successive movement from an event to its repression to its return. Yet what is truly striking about the accident victim's experience of the event and what in fact constitutes the central enigma of Freud's example, is not so much the period of forgetting that occurs after the accident, but rather the fact that the victim of the crash was never fully conscious during the accident itself: the person gets away, Freud says, "apparently unharmed." The experience of trauma, the fact of latency, would thus seem to consist, not in the forgetting of a reality that can hence never be fully known, but in an inherent latency within the experience itself. The historical power of the trauma is not just that the experience is repeated after its forgetting, but that it is only in and through its inherent forgetting that it is first experienced at all. And it is this inherent latency of the event that paradoxically explains the peculiar, temporal structure, the belatedness, of historical experience: since the traumatic event is not experienced as it occurs, it is fully evident only in connection with another place, and in another time.[12]

The analogy that Freud is drawing between the genesis of a "traumatic neurosis" and the trauma experienced as a result of the murder of Moses is one where latency is a crucial stage. Latency simultaneously involves *both* forgetting and (unconscious) remembering. This is what happens in the genesis of an individual traumatic neurosis, and, according to Freud, it is what also happened in the course of Jewish history. Without the appeal to this psychoanalytic understanding of latency it would not be possible to explain the "remarkable fact" of the gap in a religious tradition – how a tradition instead of "becoming weaker with time, became more and more powerful in the course of centuries" (23:69).

Jan Assmann provides yet another important perspective on the cultural significance of the concept of latency and the return of the repressed. In the long history of the discourse on Moses and Egypt that he so carefully explores, he tells us that:

a displacement of antagonism can be ascertained which proceeds from the outer to the inner. We start with revolution and expulsion, then proceed to secrecy and mystery, in which the antagonism takes place within one society, and end up with latency, where the antagonism resides in the individual as well as the collective soul. Latency as a third model of religious antagonism and tension is the discovery of Sigmund Freud and constitutes his most important contribution to the discourse on Moses and Egypt. Freud's great discovery and lasting contribution to this discourse is the role which he attributed to the dynamics of memory and the return of the repressed . . . one should acknowledge that the concepts of latency and the return of the repressed are indispensable for any adequate theory of cultural memory. They need, however, to be redefined in cultural terms. Freud reminded us of the fact that there is such a thing as "cultural forgetting" or even "cultural repression." Since Freud, no theory of culture can afford not to take these concepts into consideration. The old concept of tradition has proved insufficient. (*ME*, 215)

Freud's distinctive understanding of trauma and latency enables us to understand another "gap" – a gap in Freud's argument. In Freud's historical account of what happened after Moses was murdered in the wilderness, he tells us that the Levites (Moses' Egyptian retinue) kept alive the memory of Moses and the horrible deed of his murder. But if this were so, then we may ask, why do we even need to appeal to latency and trauma to account for what happened? Why do we even need to bring into the narrative any reference to unconscious memory-traces? After all, by Freud's own admission, there was a conscious oral tradition by which these memories were kept alive. Freud does not address this point directly – what might appear as not simply a "gap" in this narrative but a manifest contradiction. Yet, on the basis of what he does say, we can see what Freud might have argued. In the first place, Freud does think that this oral tradition was actively suppressed, especially when – centuries after the time when the murder of Moses occurred –

the scribes wrote down and canonized the "official" narrative history of the Exodus. More importantly, strictly speaking, the murder of Moses was *not* the decisive event in forming the Jewish tradition. Rather, it was the belated traumatic experience of this alleged event that is so crucial. Just as the "victim of the crash was never fully conscious during the accident itself," so too the witnesses of Moses' murder were not *fully conscious* of the psychic historical significance of this event. Although there are, of course, conscious symptoms and consequences of trauma, the traumatic experience is never fully *conscious*.

ORAL TRADITION

When Freud introduces his analogy between "the remarkable course of the history of the Jewish religion" and "the genesis of human neurosis" he claims that "it is very complete, and approaches identity" (23:72). But he is fully aware that there are difficulties in this analogy. Contrary to a widespread impression that Freud *unreflectively* applies individual psychology to group phenomena (and in particular to the Jewish people), he raises this problem as a fundamental difficulty in the very section entitled "Difficulties." He speaks of two problems that arise in the analogy he has drawn between "neurotic processes and religious events." The first, which he considers less important, is that he has "dealt with only a single instance from the copious phenomenology of religions and [has] thrown no light on any others" (23:92). Freud concedes that his lack of expert knowledge does not allow him to consider other religions (although he has a great deal to say about Christianity – which arises out of Judaism).[13]

It is the second difficulty that he considers far more important because it "poses a fresh problem of a fundamental nature." It "raises the question in what form the operative tradition in the life of peoples is present – a question which does not occur with individuals, since there it is solved by the existence in the unconscious of memory-traces of the past" (23:93). I stress Freud's awareness of this difficulty for two reasons. The first is that it shows that Freud himself was acutely aware that one cannot directly transfer the psychoanalytic insights gleaned from the study of neurotic individuals to group phenomena without an independent argument that justifies this analogy. The second reason is that it brings us to the explicit consideration of the character, power, and dynamics of tradition in the life of a people – and in particular, the Jewish people.

Freud introduces his discussion of tradition by speaking about it in a familiar manner. He claims that when the Semites left Egypt with their new leader Moses they brought "writing and the desire to write history along with them" (23:68). But historical writing at this time was not yet "pledged to unswerving truthfulness." There were no "scruples about shaping its narratives according to the needs and purposes of the moment." The immediate purpose, after the joining of different tribes at Kadesh, was "to glorify the new god [Yahweh] and to dispute his being foreign" (23:68).

As a result of these circumstances a discrepancy was able to grow up between the written record and the oral transmission of the same material – *tradition*. What had been omitted or changed in the written record might very well have been preserved intact in tradition. Tradition was a supplement but at the same time a contradiction to historical writing. It was less subjected to the influence of distorting purposes and perhaps at some points quite exempt from them, and it might therefore be more truthful than the account that had been recorded in writing. Its trustworthiness, however, suffered from the fact that it was less stable and definite than the written account and exposed to numerous changes and alterations when it was handed on from one generation to another by oral communication. A tradition of such a kind might meet with various sorts of fate. What we should most expect would be that it would be crushed by the written account, would be unable to stand up against it, would become more and more shadowy and would finally pass into oblivion. But it might meet with other fates: one of these would be that the tradition itself would end in a written record, and we shall have to deal with yet others as we proceed. (23:68–9)

There are several points that I want to emphasize in this initial discussion of the role of tradition. The concept of tradition that is presupposed in the above passage does not draw on any special psychoanalytic insights. Tradition here is primarily understood as oral tradition (as distinguished from written texts). Freud makes a point which has become especially significant in the recent interest in oral history. Oral tradition does not necessarily correspond with written records – and in some instances can be more "truthful" than what has been "recorded in writing." But even though oral traditions may eventually be recorded, they tend to be unstable, and can all too easily be crushed and forgotten by written accounts. Although the explicit written biblical narrative of the Exodus has come to prevail in Jewish history, there is evidence (so Freud believes) of a discrepancy between the written record and the oral tradition. (Of course, the basis for claiming that there is such a discrepancy is itself based on the alleged distortions in the written texts.) This is why Freud draws on the work of Ernst Sellin. It was Sellin who was able to detect "unmistakable signs of a tradition to the effect that Moses . . . met with a violent end in the rising of his refractory and stiff-necked people, and that at the same time the religion he had introduced was thrown off" (23:36).

Nevertheless, this concept of an oral tradition is not sufficient to explain "the remarkable fact" that after a long period of latency, the Mosaic tradition of monotheism re-asserted itself with renewed power and vigor. Anticipating the outcome of his investigation, Freud affirms that "there is an almost complete conformity in this respect between the individual and the group: in the group too an impression of the past is retained in unconscious memory-traces" (23:94). What does this mean? And how is it possible – especially in light of Freud's explicit rejection of a doctrine of a group or collective unconscious? Here we touch upon the most vital (and in my opinion) the most misunderstood aspect of Freud's reflections on tradition. Even such sympathetic interpreters as Ernest Jones, Ernst Kris and Yosef Yerushalmi (and many others) criticize Freud for clinging to a dubious doctrine of Lamarckism.

FREUD'S LAMARCKISM?

Yerushalmi sums up the prevailing criticism of Freud's alleged Lamarckism when he writes:

Nowhere is Freud's Lamarckism more striking and radical than in *Moses and Monotheism*. Even if we temporarily suspend our scientific disbelief, beguiled by Freud's own passing definition of scientific creativity as the "succession of daringly playful fantasy and relentlessly realistic criticism," the Lamarckism in *Moses and Monotheism* makes the most difficult demands on fantasy itself. For it is one thing even to imagine the formation of a phylogenetic heritage in the remotest prehistoric ages when, ostensibly, the structures of the human psyche were still in an early and fluid process of evolution, and certain overwhelming and universal experiences, repeated again and again over enormous periods of time, eventually left psychological imprints that could somehow be transmitted somatically to future generations.

Here, however, trauma in the form of a unique cluster of historical events, their encoding within the genetic legacy of a particular group, collective repression, and the "return of the repressed" all take place in relatively recent historical time within the brief span of some five to eight centuries. Moreover, not only the traumatic slaying of Moses, but the content of his religious teaching is alleged to have undergone this fateful and intricate process. The archaic heritage of human beings, Freud insists in *Moses and Monotheism,* "comprises not only dispositions but subject matter – memory-traces of the experience of earlier generations." At which point even the most ardent and loyal admirer of Freud can only whisper to himself, "Certum, quia absurdum est." (*FM,* 30–31)

If Yerushalmi were correct, this would be a devastating criticism. It would mean that Freud failed to solve what he himself called a "problem of a fundamental nature." It would call into question the basis for Freud's entire study – the analogy that he draws between the development of a neurosis in an individual and the development of what occurred to the Jewish people in the course of their history.

But Yerushalmi is mistaken, or so I want to argue. He misrepresents the subtlety of Freud's argument. We have to confront directly the criticism that Freud bases his understanding of Jewish history on a "discredited" Lamarckism, in order to bring out the nuances of his understanding of the dynamics of a religious tradition. This requires a detailed analysis of those passages in *The Man Moses and the Monotheistic Religion* which presumably warrant the claim that Freud's Lamarckism is "striking and radical."

In this book, I have restricted myself to an analysis of the role of Freud's alleged Lamarckism or psycho-Lamarckism in *The Man Moses and the Monotheistic Religion.* I am convinced, however, that the entire question of Freud's "Lamarckism" needs to be re-opened. It has become a virtual dogma of most commentators on Freud that he was a Lamarckian. But very few have taken the trouble to clarify what *precisely* is meant by this claim. The general formula: "acquired characteristics are phylogenetically inherited" is itself excessively vague because this formula obscures the issue of *how* such "acquired characters" are transmitted – which biological and/or psychological mechanisms are involved, especially in human beings. Furthermore, Freud *never* directly refers to Lamarck in *any* of his published psychoanalytic writings.

There are several different questions that need to be carefully distinguished: What is meant by Lamarckism? What are the actual claims and theses of Lamarck himself? What is the relation between Freud's understanding of Lamarckism and the claims of Lamarck? And, to what extent does Freud *actually* base his own distinctive theses about the transmission of the archaic heritage on questionable Lamarckian assumptions?

There is also a more general question. Even if it is granted that Freud himself did hold Lamarckian beliefs, we can ask whether these are necessary for psychoanalysis. Does psychoanalysis itself presuppose Lamarckian assumptions? Many of Freud's closest psychoanalytic associates including Heinz Hartmann, Ernest Jones, Ernst Kris, and Rudolf Loewenstein did think that Freud held Lamarckian beliefs, but they also vigorously maintained that psychoanalytic findings were independent of any dubious Lamarckian assumptions. Concerning Freud's Lamarckism, Hartmann writes:

Freud draws partly on phylogeny, and more specifically on the inheritance of acquired characteristics, which would account for phenomena such as the occurrence of sexual symbols and – to mention only the most controversial instance – the occurrence of the Oedipal conflict. His views on this matter remained unchanged. When he became aware of the fact that biological studies had not confirmed Lamarckian assumptions (though strictly speaking they were not invalidated), he "postulated" the phylogenetic explanation "for psychological reasons."[14]

Ritvo, who cites this passage from Hartmann, points out that Hartmann himself "exhibits a clear evolutionary foundation, free of teleology and neo-Lamarckism. He seems to accept natural selection and the non-inheritability of acquired characteristics in the biological field as completely compatible with the requirements of psychoanalytic findings."[15]

Furthermore, even at the stage of his career (1916) when Freud was considering writing a work on Lamarck with Sándor Ferenczi (a project that was later abandoned), he had a very idiosyncratic idea of Lamarckism. In a letter to Karl Abraham which describes the project he writes:

Our intention is to base Lamarck's ideas completely on our own theories and to show that his concept of 'need', which creates and modifies organs, is nothing else than the power unconscious ideas have over the body of which we see the remains in hysteria – in short, the 'omnipotence of thoughts'. Fitness [*Zweckmässigkeit*] would then be really explained psychoanalytically; it would be the completion of psychoanalysis. Two great principles of change (of progress) would emerge: one through adaptation of one's own body, the later one through alteration of the outer world (autoplastic and heteroplastic).[16]

But let us carefully pursue the question of Freud's alleged Lamarckism in *The Man Moses and the Monotheistic Religion*. I completely agree with Derrida who, with explicit reference to Yerushalmi, questions the accuracy of this accusation. Referring to the "Difficulties" section of Part III of *The Man Moses and the Monotheistic Religion*, Derrida writes:

[Freud] repeats here that this topic has nothing to do with the anatomy of the brain, and this is enough to complicate the phylogenetic dimension, which he judges to be in effect irreducible but which he is far from simplifying in its

Lamarckian schemas (he is often accused of this, by Yerushalmi also), or even its Darwinian ones. The adherence to a biological doctrine of acquired characters – of the biological archive, in sum – cannot be made to agree in a simple and immediate way with all Freud acknowledges otherwise: the memory of the experience of previous generations, the time of the formation of languages and of a symbolicity that transcends given languages and discursivity as such. Freud is careful. He knows and recognizes explicitly "the present attitude of biological science, which refuses to hear of the inheritance of acquired characters by succeeding generations." And if he admits that it is difficult for him to do without a reference to biological evolution (and who could seriously reproach him for that, in principle and absolutely? in the name of what?), he shows himself in this regard to be more reserved and more circumspect than is usually acknowledged, distinguishing notably between acquired characters ("which are hard to grasp") and "memory-traces of external events." These characters and these traces could well follow (Freud would certainly not say it here in this form) quite complicated linguistic, cultural, cipherable, and in general ciphered transgenerational and transindividual relays, transiting thus through an archive, the science of which is not at a standstill. This does not necessarily bring us back to Lamarck or to Darwin, even if it obliges us to articulate the history of genetic programs and ciphers on all the symbolic and individual archives differently. All that Freud says is that we are receptive to an analogy between the two types of transgenerational memory or archive (the memory of an ancestral experience or the so-called biologically acquired character) and that "we cannot imagine [*vorstellen*] one without the other." Without the irrepressible, that is to say, only suppressible and repressible, force and authority of this transgenerational memory, the problems of which we speak would be dissolved and resolved in advance. There would no longer be any essential history of culture, there would no longer be any question of memory and of archive, of patriarchive or of matriarchive, and one would no longer even understand how an ancestor can speak within us, nor what sense there might be in us to speak *to* him or her, to speak in such an *unheimlich*, "uncanny" fashion, to his or her ghost. *With* it. (*AF*, 34–6)[17]

The reason why it is so important to analyze carefully the criticism that Freud bases his understanding of the dynamics of a religious tradition on a "discredited" Lamarckism, is because this has been one of the main obstacles blocking our understanding of what Freud means by a tradition, and what psychoanalysis can contribute to deepening our appreciation of the dynamics and power of religious traditions. To understand this, our initial task is to clarify the fundamental difficulty with which Freud is grappling.

Standard accounts of tradition focus on the specific means – the narratives, storytelling, rituals, and ceremonies by which a tradition is shaped and handed down from one generation to another. Freud is

certainly aware of this dimension of tradition. He calls attention to the
ways in which an oral tradition can clash with written records and even
be more "truthful" than a written record. But there are two reasons why
this concept of tradition is not sufficient to account for what happened in
the course of Jewish history. The first is that it fails to account for the
"gap" – the long period of latency – when the Mosaic religion of
monotheism was suppressed and repressed, before it eventually proved
triumphant. Phrasing the issue more generally, the problem that needs
to be confronted is to explain the discontinuity and reversal of a religious
tradition (as well as its continuity). How are we to account for the fact
that a tradition can seem to die and then "suddenly" re-assert itself?
Traditions are not simply continuous; they involve ruptures and rever-
sals. They may seem to be moribund – only to come to life again with
renewed psychological vigor. The second reason why "traditional"
accounts of tradition are inadequate is that they fail to account for the
power and intensity with which a long dormant religious tradition can
re-assert itself. Freud claims that this is what happened with the monotheism that was given to the Jews by the powerful Moses. This renewed
intensity of dormant elements is a characteristic phenomenon of many
traditions. What are the psychological dispositions of human beings
which help to explain why and how they are receptive and *resistant* to the
vicissitudes of a religious tradition? "Traditional" accounts of tradition
which restrict themselves to the conscious mental processes fail to shed
any light on the *unconscious* dynamics involved in receptivity and resistance to tradition. In his 1935 letter to Lou Andreas-Salomé that we
have cited, Freud succinctly states his main thesis:

As a half-extinguished tradition the religion of Moses had finally triumphed.
This process is typical of the way a religion is created and was only the
repetition of an earlier process. Religions owe their compulsive power to the
return of the repressed; they are reawakened memories of very ancient, forgotten,
highly emotional episodes of human history. I have already said this in *Totem
and Taboo*; I express it now in the formula: the strength of religion lies not in its
material, but in its *historical* truth. (*SFLA*, 205; Appendix, p. 118).

We have seen that Freud does *not* claim that the monotheistic religion
of Moses was totally obliterated. It was "a half-extinguished tradition"
that left its traces. His entire argument depends on the fact that there
were always memory-traces of this monotheism (as well as memory-
traces of Moses' murder). In addition to the evidence that he draws
upon from Sellin, Freud (who profoundly admires the Jewish prophetic

tradition) argues that the Prophets kept alive the Mosaic ideals. He never expresses any doubts about the authenticity of the prophetic tradition. He also mentions several important respects in which "the later god of the Jews became in the end like the old Mosaic god. The first and decisive point is that he was truly acknowledged as the only god, beside whom any other god was unthinkable" (23:64). Furthermore "[t]he voices of the Prophets never tired of declaring that God despised ceremonial and sacrifice and required only that people should believe in him and lead a life in truth and justice. And when they praised the simplicity and holiness of life in the wilderness they were certainly under the influence of the Mosaic ideals" (23:64).

In a passage where Freud's pride in his Jewish heritage shines through, he writes:

[I]t would obviously be unjust to break off the chain of causes at Moses and to neglect what was effected by those who succeeded him and carried on his ideas, the Jewish Prophets. The seed of monotheism failed to ripen in Egypt. The same thing might have happened in Israel after the people had thrown off the burdensome and exacting religion. But there constantly arose from the Jewish people men who revived the fading tradition, who renewed the admonitions and demands made by Moses, and who did not rest till what was lost had been established once again. In the course of constant efforts over centuries, and finally owing to two great reforms, one before and one after the Babylonian exile, the transformation was accomplished of the popular god Yahweh into the God whose worship had been forced upon the Jews by Moses. And evidence of the presence of a peculiar psychical aptitude in the masses who had become the Jewish people is revealed by the fact that they were able to produce so many individuals prepared to take on the burdens of the religion of Moses in return for the reward of being the chosen people and perhaps for some other prizes of a similar degree. (23:111)

There is no suggestion of any Lamarckism here. Freud (as Derrida perceptively observes) is alluding to the fact that there are "memory-traces" of the Mosaic ideals in the prophetic tradition. Concerning Freud's alleged Lamarckism, it should be noted that Freud himself never refers to Lamarck in *The Man Moses and the Monotheistic Religion*, although he does mention Darwin several times.[18]

What precisely is meant by Freud's Lamarckism? It is helpful to introduce a heuristic distinction between "strong" and "weak" Lamarckism. By strong (or strict) Lamarckism, I mean the doctrine that acquired characteristics of an individual or species are biologically (genetically) transmitted to future generations. When Yerushalmi speaks of a "unique cluster of historical events" which is *encoded* in the "genetic legacy of a particular group" he employs a concept of strong Lamarckism. But at times – especially when Yerushalmi speaks of Freud's "psycho-Lamarckism" – he seems to be utilizing a much weaker and more open-ended conception of Lamarckism; where decisive experiences in the history of a people shape the psychological character of future generations. But this so-called "psycho-Lamarckism" does not make any explicit claim about *how* these decisive experiences are transmitted.[19] Because it is primarily Freud's remarks in the "Difficulties" section that have been taken as a basis for claiming that he is committed to a "radical" Lamarckism, I want to examine what Freud says (and does not say) here.

DIFFICULTIES

Freud's account of the events leading up to the compromise that (he claims) took place at Kadesh does not present any special problems concerning the role of tradition. "According to our theory, a tradition of this kind was based on conscious memories of oral communications which people then living had received from their ancestors only two or three generations back who had themselves been participants and eye-witnesses of the events in question" (23:93). Nevertheless, the "fresh problem" that Freud needs to solve arises when one can no longer appeal to a "knowledge normally handed on from grandfather to grandchild" (23:93). According to Sellin, knowledge of the murder of Moses was always kept within priestly circles. Consequently, it was known only by a few people. What about the ordinary people – the "masses"? "It seems, rather, as though there must have been something present in the ignorant masses, too, which was in some way akin to the knowledge of the few and went half way to meet it when it was uttered" (23:94). Freud's phrasing here does not entail a doctrine of strong Lamarckism. He speaks about what is *known* by the "masses" that enables them to understand what the priestly class "utters." He does not assert that this "knowledge" has been biologically transmitted. Freud does draw an analogy between the individual and the group when he says "in the group too an impression of the past is retained in unconscious memory-traces" (23:94). But he does *not* say that these "unconscious memory-traces" are genetically encoded. Freud then presents a highly condensed version of his theory of the unconscious, preconscious and conscious; repression; and the topographical theory of id, ego, and super-ego. He stresses (as Derrida has noted) that "the psychical top-ography that I have developed here has nothing to do with the anatomy of the brain . . ." (23:97). He even speaks of "our complete ignorance of the *dynamic* nature of mental processes" (23:97). This admission is important because it shows how Freud is acutely aware (even near the end of his life) of how ignorant we still remain about the dynamics of our conscious and unconscious mental processes – including the complex ways in which unconscious mental processes and memory-traces are transmitted and shape our conscious lives. Unconscious mental processes are not *totally* sealed off from our conscious lives; they are always affecting and shaping them, albeit in devious and complex ways.

Freud notes, however, that a "fresh complication arises when we become aware of the probability that what may be operative in an individual's psychical life may include not only what he has experienced himself but also things that were innately present in him at his birth, elements with a phylogenetic origin – an *archaic heritage*. The questions then arise of what this consists in, what it contains and what is the evidence for it" (23:98). If one were looking for evidence of "strong" Lamarckism, one might cite this passage as clear evidence. But such a conclusion would be too hasty. The hypothesis that there are constitut-ive elements of a phylogenetic origin in individuals and species is not in itself especially controversial. Elements of a phylogenetic origin consist "in certain [innate] dispositions such as are characteristic of all living organisms: in the capacity and tendency, that is, to enter particular lines of development and to react in a particular manner to certain excita-tions, impressions, and stimuli" (23:98). This general thesis is at least as old as Aristotle who argued that we can characterize different species by the potentialities which they can actualize, for example, human beings are animals who have the potentiality to speak – a potentiality that can only be actualized or realized when they are taught to do so. When Aristotle introduces the distinction between primary innate potentiali-ties and secondary acquired potentialities, he introduces a conceptual distinction that is helpful for clarifying what Freud means. For example, it is a primary potentiality of human animals to be able to learn a language. This general capacity enables us to learn specific languages. When we have learned to speak a language (for example, Greek) but are not *actually* speaking it, we have acquired a new secondary potentiality – one which is, of course, dependent on the generic human capacity to learn and to speak a language. The claim that there are determinate psychological dispositions is the basis for Freud's entire psychoanalytic understanding of the individual. Each of us is born with a set of dispositions that shape our individual contingent psychic lives and development. The way in which these are experienced in our individual lives depends on all sorts of unpredictable contingencies.

Freud also claims that the phenomenon of universal symbolism in language does give one "cause for thought." As early as *The Interpretation of Dreams*, Freud argued that there is an ubiquity of symbolism which transcends individual languages and cannot be explained as a form of learned behavior. He tells us that "symbolism disregards differences of language; investigations would probably show that it is ubiquitous – the same for all peoples. Here then, we seem to have an assured instance of an archaic heritage dating from the period at which language developed" (23:99).

It is certainly difficult to give an explanation of how human beings have acquired such universal symbols, symbols which occur in our dreams and which we frequently do not understand unless an analyst interprets them. Frankly, I do not think that Freud ever did explain how we acquire these universal symbols. But I am not claiming that Freud gave such an account. This is not the primary issue (in the context of my argument). Rather, the specific issue we are examining is whether (and in what sense) Freud is a Lamarckian. Thus far, nothing that Freud says presupposes or entails "strong" Lamarckism. Freud, of course, is claiming that there are determinate "intellectual dispositions" just as there are "instinctual dispositions." Of course, we do need to inquire whether he has correctly identified such dispositions, what evidence he gives to support his hypotheses, and how we are to account for the genesis of these dispositions. But giving an account of the genesis of specific dispositions (instinctual or intellectual) is required for *any* adequate biological theory of evolution – including Darwin's.[20] Freud himself indicates that he is aware of the possibility of alternative explanations of the "origin" of such symbolism. In the sentence immediately following his claim that here "we seem to have an assured instance of an archaic heritage dating from the period at which language developed," he writes:

But another explanation might still be attempted. It might be said that we are dealing with thought-connections between ideas – connections which had been established during the historical development of speech and which have to be repeated now every time the development of speech has to be gone through in an individual. It would thus be a case of the inheritance of an intellectual disposition similar to the ordinary inheritance of an instinctual disposition – and once again it would be no contribution to our problem. (23:99)

Freud next takes up the question of the study of traumas which "exceeds in its importance what we have so far considered" (23:99).

When we study the reactions to early traumas, we are quite often surprised to find that they are not strictly limited to what the subject himself has really experienced but diverge from it in a way which fits in much better with the model of a phylogenetic event and, in general, can only be explained by such an influence. The behaviour of neurotic children towards their parents in the Oedipus and castration complex abounds in such reactions, which seem unjustified in the individual case and only become intelligible phylogenetically – by their connection with the experience of earlier generations. (23:99)

Freud ventures "on a further step" and posits "the assertion that the archaic heritage of human beings comprises not only dispositions but also subject-matter – memory-traces of the experience of earlier genera-tions" (23:99). This is the sentence that Yerushalmi cites when he declares "even the most ardent and loyal admirer of Freud can only whisper to himself, 'Certum, quia absurdum est'" (*FM*, 31).

It is the following passage that has been taken to be the decisive evidence that Freud refused to abandon his "discredited" Lamarckism. I want to cite the relevant paragraphs in their entirety, before analyzing them.

On further reflection I must admit that I have behaved for a long time as though the inheritance of memory-traces of the experience of our ancestors, independently of direct communication and of the influence of education by the setting of an example, were established beyond question. When I spoke of the survival of a tradition among a people or of the formation of a people's character, I had mostly in mind an inherited tradition of this kind and not one transmitted by communication. Or at least I made no distinction between the two and was not clearly aware of my audacity in neglecting to do so. My position, no doubt, is made more difficult by the present attitude of biological science, which refuses to hear of the inheritance of acquired characters by succeeding generations. I must, however, in all modesty confess that neverthe-less I cannot do without this factor in biological evolution. The same thing is not in question, indeed, in the two cases: in one it is a matter of acquired characters which are hard to grasp, in the other of memory-traces of external events – something tangible, as it were. But it may well be that at bottom we cannot imagine one without the other.

If we assume the survival of these memory-traces in the archaic heritage, we have bridged the gulf between individual and group psychology: we can deal with peoples as we do with an individual neurotic. Granted that at the time we have no stronger evidence for the presence of memory-traces in the archaic heritage than the residual phenomena of the work of analysis which call for a phylogenetic derivation, yet this evidence seems to us strong enough to postu-late that such is the fact. If it is not so, we shall not advance a step further along the path we entered on, either in analysis or in group psychology. The audacity cannot be avoided. (23:99–100)

I want to call attention to the rhetoric of these two paragraphs. Freud begins with a *self-criticism* of his former beliefs. He acknowledges that he behaved as if the inheritance of memory-traces independent of direct communication was "beyond question." He even acknowledges that he had failed to make a distinction between a tradition inherited by memory-traces and one transmitted by direct communication. At the very least then, Freud shows his awareness that there is a problem concerning "the inheritance of memory-traces of the experience of our ancestors." Furthermore, in these passages Freud speaks of his "mod-esty" and "audacity." Freud does say – as Derrida has noted – that he "modestly confesses" that he cannot do without "the inheritance of acquired characters by succeeding generations" but he does not take a firm position here on how such acquired characters are transmitted. This, as I have indicated, is the decisive issue, if one is to ascribe a doctrine of "strong" Lamarckism to Freud. Furthermore – and this is even more important – Freud does *not* assimilate the "memory-traces of external events" (such as the memory-traces of the murder of Moses) to "acquired characters which are hard to grasp." He sharply distinguishes between these, although he hedges his claims when he suggests that "it may well be that at bottom we cannot imagine one without the other." The key issue for Freud in understanding what has happened in the course of Jewish history is *not* the "inheritance of acquired characters by succeeding generations." It is rather the issue of "the presence of memory-traces in the archaic heritage" – or more accurately how (unconscious) "memory-traces of external events" are transmitted. It is certainly true that without the "audacious" postulate that such transmission does take place "we shall not advance a step further along the path we entered on, either in analysis or in group psychology," but it is still an open question as to how this transgenerational transmission takes place.

Let me step back for a moment and clarify what I am claiming (and not claiming) – and why. I do not want to deny that Freud had (in some sense) Lamarckian proclivities in his understanding of evolution; that he did believe that there is "the inheritance of acquired characters by succeeding generations." I have been arguing that we need to be *precise* about what exactly Freud is claiming and presupposing in *The Man*

Moses and the Monotheistic Religion. I have carefully analyzed the relevant passages in order to demonstrate that Freud's alleged Lamarckism is not "striking" or "radical" in the way in which Yerushalmi (and others) indicate. Freud does not say, presuppose, or imply that "trauma in the form of a unique cluster of historical events" is encoded "within the genetic legacy of a particular group." This is why I think that Derrida is right when he affirms that Freud is more careful than those who criticize him for presupposing a discredited Lamarckism, and that this accusation obscures Freud's contribution to our understanding of tradition and the essential history of culture.

Let me turn once more to the controversial sentence which has been taken as indisputable evidence that Freud is advocating a strong Lamarckism: "My position, no doubt, is made more difficult by the present attitude of biological science, which refuses to hear of the inheritance of acquired characters of succeeding generations." I want to offer an alternative reading which is not only compatible with what Freud says in the *Moses* book, but also fits much better with Freud's understanding of the scientific spirit of psychoanalysis. I suggest that Freud is seeking to clarify the conditions that an adequate theory of biological evolution must satisfy – the phenomena it must explain, not *explain away*. What psychoanalysis has discovered – according to Freud – is that there are certain basic psychological dispositions and characteristics. For example, there are basic psychological dispositions such as the Oedipus complex and the castration complex which presuppose unconscious mental processes such as repression and defense mechanisms. No two individuals experience the Oedipus complex in quite the same way. This leaves plenty of room for chance and contingency. Furthermore, these psychological dispositions did not always exist; they have a genealogy. But once they do come into existence, they are transmitted to future generations. They become "a constitutional factor of the individual." Freud is certainly aware that such a genealogy takes place over a long period of time. It is this genealogy, the emergence of these distinctive psychological dispositions, processes, and characteristics that must eventually be explained by an adequate theory of evolution. These are "acquired characters"; they have emerged in the course of human evolution. Freud as a psychoanalyst is specifying the phenomena that are to be explained by an adequate theory of biological evolution – what philosophers call the explicandum. Ironically, it is Freud who seeks to expose the type of dogmatism that would rule out the very possibility of the emergence of psychological dispositions which are transmitted to

succeeding generations (the Oedipus complex) because they are presumably incompatible with our current theories of biological evolution.
This would surely block the road of open scientific inquiry.

Sometimes it seems as if those who criticize Freud for his alleged
Lamarckism are reasoning in the following manner. If one claims that
there is a "survival of . . . memory-traces in the archaic heritage," then
this survival can be explained in one of two ways: *either* it occurs because
of a *conscious* handing down of a tradition (stories, parables, examples,
etc.) *or* this "information" is genetically encoded and thereby transmitted. Freud denies the first alternative so he is forced to adopt the second
(Lamarckian) alternative. But such a line of reasoning misses the main
point of Freud's subtle analysis. For there is a third possibility – the one
that Freud is struggling to articulate – one in which we can speak of the
survival and transmission of *unconscious* memory-traces.

TRADITION: THE INTERPLAY OF CONSCIOUS AND UNCONSCIOUS MEMORY-TRACES

One of the reasons why it is difficult to accept Freud's claim that there
are unconscious memory-traces is because of a failure to understand
what Freud means by conscious and unconscious mental processes.
There is a misguided tendency to think of the unconscious in a reified
manner – as some sort of "container" which is totally separated from
consciousness. But this is not Freud's conception of the unconscious.
The unconscious – or more accurately, unconscious mental processes –
is always affecting our consciousness, albeit in hidden, devious, and
distorted ways. It is these traces – these marks left on our consciousness –
that are the very basis for postulating unconscious mental processes. In
his classic paper, "The Unconscious," Freud poses the question:

How are we to arrive at a knowledge of the unconscious? It is of course only as
something conscious that we know it, after it has undergone transformation or
translation into something conscious. Psycho-analytic work shows us every day
that translation of this kind is possible. (14:166)

Moreover, in *An Outline of Psycho-analysis* (written after the *Moses* study),
where Freud attempted "to bring together the tenets of psycho-analysis
and to state them, as it were, dogmatically – in the most concise form
and in the most unequivocal terms" (23:144), he writes:

We have discovered technical methods of filling up the gaps in the phenomena of
our consciousness, and we make use of those methods just as a physicist makes

use of experiment. In this manner we infer a number of processes which are in themselves 'unknowable' and interpolate them in those that are conscious to us. And if, for instance, we say: 'At this point an unconscious memory intervened', what that means is: 'At this point something occurred of which we are totally unable to form a conception, but which, if it had entered our consciousness, could only have been described in such and such a way.' (23:196–7)

The great contribution of psychoanalysis has been to teach us that not all communication – and sometimes not even the most important communication – takes place by conscious mental activities. There is "always already" unconscious communication in any social interaction. It is exactly this unconscious communication that is most vital to the understanding of psychoanalytic therapy. In Freud's famous papers on psychoanalytic technique, he stresses that just as the "first rule of psychoanalysis" is to encourage the patient to refrain from self-censorship, there is a complement to this rule for the analyst. "[He] must bend his own unconscious like a receptive organ towards the emerging unconscious of the patient" (12:115). Without this communication between the unconscious of the patient and the unconscious of the therapist, psychoanalytic therapy would not be possible. In short, Freud maintains that communication that takes place between human beings is *never* exhausted by what is consciously and explicitly communicated. This is not only true among contemporaries but also in the transgenerational communication that constitutes a living tradition.

What is communicated from one generation to the next is not only what is explicitly stated or what is set forth by precept and example, but also what is unconsciously communicated. Unless we pay attention to these unconscious dynamics of transmission, we will never understand the receptivity (and resistance) to a living tradition. What is repressed in the memory of a people is never "totally" repressed in the sense of being hermetically sealed off from their conscious lives; there are always unconscious memory-traces of what has been repressed. This is why there can be a "return of the repressed," a return that can break out with great psychic force in an individual or in the history of a people.

Raising the specter of "strong Lamarckism" obscures what is most original, audacious and thought-provoking in Freud's reflections on the Jewish religious tradition. Although I have sought to refute the accusation that there is a "striking and radical" Lamarckism in *The Man Moses and the Monotheistic Religion*, this has not been the primary reason for my close analysis of the "Difficulties" section. My intention has been to make a positive point about Freud's contribution to our understanding

of the ways in which a tradition is handed down. Freud is expanding and
deepening our conception of a religious tradition – especially the Jewish
religious tradition. He is fully aware of the complex modalities by which
a tradition is consciously handed down – by examples, stories, precepts,
rituals, commandments, etc. But in considering these conscious modalities, we must also be aware of what is also unconsciously communicated
and repressed. Although Freud does not quite put it this way, we might
say that there are both conscious and unconscious memory-traces which
interplay with each other in the transmission of a tradition. In drawing
the analogy between the dynamics of traumatic neurosis in the individual and the role of trauma in the history of a people, Freud is focusing
our attention on this interplay of conscious and unconscious memory-
traces. In the patriarchal Jewish religious tradition, there are not only
the memory-traces of the slaying of Moses but also memory-traces of the
killing of the primal father. This is why Freud says: "I have no hesitation
in declaring that men have always known (in this special way) that they
once possessed a primal father and killed him" (23:101). This forgotten
memory (so Freud claims) became active once again with the traumatic
event when the Jews killed Moses. We can see how removed Freud's
thinking is from any doctrine of "strong Lamarckism" when he writes:

Two further questions must now be answered. First, under what conditions
does a memory of this kind enter the archaic heritage? And, secondly, in what
circumstances can it become active – that is, can it advance to consciousness
from its unconscious state in the id, even though in an altered and distorted
shape? The answer to the first question is easy to formulate: the memory enters
the archaic heritage if the event was important enough, or repeated often
enough, or both. In the case of parricide both conditions are fulfilled. On the
second question there is this to be said. A whole number of influences may be
concerned, not all of which are necessarily known. A spontaneous development
is also conceivable, on the analogy of what happens in some neuroses. *What is
certainly of decisive importance, however, is the awakening of the forgotten memory-trace by a
recent real repetition of the event.* The murder of Moses was a repetition of this kind
and, later, the supposed judicial murder of Christ: so that these events come
into the foreground as causes. It seems as though the genesis of monotheism
could not do without these occurrences. We are reminded of the poet's words:

> Was unsterblich im Gesang soll leben,
> Muss im Leben untergehn.   (23:101, emphasis added)[21]

This passage underscores why Freud has put so much emphasis on the
"fact" that Moses was murdered by the Jews. It reminds us of what
Freud said earlier about trauma where its effects are of two kinds,

positive and negative. The positive effect is the remembrance of the event that has been forgotten – "to make it real, to experience a repetition of it anew" (23:75). The traumatic effect of the murder of Moses is a repetition which provokes the memory of the murder of the primal father. But there is not only repetition and remembrance of the forgotten experience. There is also the negative effect of trauma – the repression of the trauma. The aim of these negative reactions is "that nothing of the forgotten traumas shall be remembered and nothing repeated" (23:76). This double contradictory "logic" stands at the core of Freud's theory of trauma – whether it is the trauma that triggers neurosis in the life of an individual or the traumatic events that generate a religious tradition. Trauma is both affirmative and negative; it involves both remembering and forgetting. In repression itself there is an encrypting of an unconscious memory.

There are many strands in Freud's reflections of the concept of a religious tradition and the complex ways in which it is transmitted. At this stage of our analysis it may be helpful to pause and to stand back in order to highlight what Freud has contributed to our understanding of a religious tradition – and more generally to the concept of tradition. One of my primary claims has been that the meaning of a religious tradition stands at the very center of *The Man Moses and the Monotheistic Religion*.

In the twentieth century several independent lines of inquiry have led to a reconsideration of the meaning of tradition and the role that it plays in our everyday lives. Some argue that this concern is a response to the ways in which the technological processes of modernization threaten tradition. Some stress that the growth of historical consciousness (especially in the nineteenth century) compel us to rethink what tradition means. Still others are sharply critical of the biases against tradition that have been so deeply entrenched in modern thought. One of the outstanding thinkers of our time who has focused attention on the recovery of tradition has been the German philosopher, Hans-Georg Gadamer. In his magnum opus, *Truth and Method*, Gadamer draws on the entire tradition of Western philosophy in order to elucidate the meaning of tradition.[22] Imaginatively appropriating the reflections of Hegel, Husserl, and Heidegger, Gadamer argues that something dramatically new has been achieved in the twentieth century. Primarily because of Heidegger's insights in *Being and Time*, we have come to appreciate the *ontological* significance of tradition. The traditions to which we belong not only influence and shape who we are – they are *constitutive* of our very being-in-the-world. As Gadamer is fond of declaring, we "always already" belong to traditions before they belong to us. To elucidate and justify this striking ontological claim, Gadamer criticizes what he calls the "Enlightenment prejudice against prejudice." Prejudices (prejudgments) are not merely negative, blind, or the result of hastiness and superstition. There are *enabling* prejudices or prejudgments. These prejudgments are themselves embodied and handed down in the traditions that constitute what we are. Of course, it is a constant critical task to distinguish those prejudices or prejudgments that are enabling from those which distort our understanding. But it is an illusion to think that it is even possible to free ourselves from all prejudices and prejudgments. In this respect, Gadamer is sharply critical of the Cartesian bias which has influenced so much of modern thought. Without the prejudgments inherited from the traditions that shape us, we would never be able to encounter and understand the world in a meaningful way. Tradition is not to be thought of as the dead weight of the past. There is (and ought to be) an ongoing open *critical dialogue* with the traditions to which we belong. This is the way in which a tradition is kept alive – by being creatively reinterpreted. A living tradition is not based on blind obedience. This is a caricature of tradition. Rather tradition is based upon the claim to *knowledge*. Furthermore, Gadamer criticizes the idea that tradition stands opposed to reason. Reason itself becomes effective when it is historically embodied in tradition. We must always try to keep ourselves open and respond with hermeneutic sensitivity to the "claim to truth" that tradition makes upon us. As finite human beings we are limited by our own horizons, but we aspire to achieve a "fusion of horizons" in our dialogical encounters with tradition. So a tradition is not something that is past, it is also present in determining who we are. A tradition demands a response from us. And there is also a future dimension to tradition insofar as it is essentially open to reinterpretation in light of future experience and new horizons that arise.

Gadamer is certainly not alone in making these forceful claims about tradition. Alasdair MacIntyre, Charles Taylor, Martha Nussbaum, Paul Ricoeur (and many others) have also argued for the ontological character of tradition – the complex ways in which traditions (even conflicting traditions) define who we are and who we aspire to be. Although they sharply disagree with each other on many issues, they all affirm that a hermeneutically sensitive understanding of the concept of tradition transforms our orientation toward the entire range of philosophic questions. Our understanding of knowledge, self, identity, morality, and politics are all transformed. We gain a new appreciation of the role of narrative and storytelling in our everyday lives and in the human disciplines. There is scarcely a discipline, from the philosophy of science through the humanities and social sciences, to the study of psychological development, that has not been seriously affected by the recovery of the concept of tradition. There is another theme shared by these thinkers. We need, to use the Freudian idiom, to appreciate the *preconscious* dimension of tradition. There is much more to any vital tradition than lies within our field of consciousness. Traditions themselves are determined by background cultural practices that are not consciously present to us. The hermeneutical task of the human sciences – as Gadamer characterizes it – is to strive to bring to consciousness what has been preconscious. This is the way in which we at once come to understand a tradition and ourselves. For self-knowledge can only be achieved in and through this hermeneutic appropriation of tradition. There can be no finality to the ongoing dialogue with tradition. In this sense all understanding and interpretation is at once *terminable* (because of our limited finite horizons) and *interminable* (because we can never anticipate the ways in which future horizons will require a reinterpretation of what is past). Gadamer is not exclusively concerned with what is distinctive about a *religious* tradition, but his reflections on tradition are applicable to all traditions including scientific and religious traditions.

Against this background we can appreciate what is so revolutionary in Freud's thinking. There is a great deal that Freud shares with this recovery of the concept of tradition. We have seen this in the way in which he explores oral traditions and their interplay with traditions that become canonized into written texts. He would, however, be extremely critical of those attempts to employ the concept of tradition in order to call into question the universality of science and reason – especially the science of psychoanalysis. In this respect Freud is a true and dedicated scion of the Enlightenment. But Freud shows us that we need to transform our understanding of a religious tradition in a revolutionary way with the psychoanalytic understanding of the dynamics of the unconscious. What is most vital in a tradition is not just what is *preconscious*, but what is genuinely *unconscious*. An adequate understanding of tradition requires us to account for the gaps and ruptures in the transmission of tradition. We need to acknowledge that what is transmitted in the handing down of a tradition is not always what is consciously and directly communicated. We cannot even adequately grasp what is directly communicated unless we also understand how it is affected and frequently distorted by dynamic unconscious processes.

We need to understand the long periods of "latency," the ways in which traditions can reassert themselves with tremendous psychic power, the role that "traumas" play in the life of a people, the complex interplay of collective forgetting and remembering, the unconscious psychic dispositions that make people receptive and resistant to traditions. We must dig deeper and discover what Derrida calls "the psychoanalytic archive," and the traces of unconscious memories. Most fundamentally, the cultural dynamics of the "return of the repressed" must be grasped if we are to comprehend the vicissitudes and compulsive power of a religious tradition.

I do not want to claim that Freud has a fully developed theory of a religious tradition, or that he has even adequately worked out and worked through the analogies he makes between psychological patterns in neurotic individuals and in collective groups. At times, *The Man Moses and the Monotheistic Religion* reads more like the juxtaposition of oddly shaped brilliant fragments rather than anything resembling a coherent theory. But one measure of the significance of an original thinker is the fertility of his insights. By this criterion, Freud has revolutionized the way in which we think about tradition and cultural memory. We are still assimilating, appropriating, and developing Freud's insights. The creative appropriation of Freudian concepts and insights, in the burgeoning interest in cultural memory and forgetting, is itself an indication of the belated fertility of Freud's thinking. This is why I so completely agree with Jan Assmann's emphatic assertion which I have previously cited: "Since Freud, no theory of culture can afford not to take these concepts into consideration. The old concept of tradition has proved insufficient" (*ME*, 215).

But there is a question that haunts us. We may still feel that Freud, in his historical reconstruction of the origins and development of monotheism, has, at best, told us a likely story. He has created an elaborate fiction, given expression to a personal fantasy, created his own myth, or built "a magnificent castle in the air." What does this have to do with "truth"? What does Freud even mean by the formula that he keeps repeating, "the strength of religion lies not in its *material* truth, but in its *historical* truth"?

HISTORICAL TRUTH

The penultimate section of Part III of *The Man Moses and the Monotheistic Religion* is entitled "Historical Truth." If we are to understand what

Freud means by historical truth, then we must return to the very beginning – not just to the beginning of the published version of the *Moses* book, but to Freud's 1934 manuscript draft. Freud originally entitled his 1934 draft, *Der Mann Moses, Ein historischer Roman* (The Man Moses: An Historical Novel). In his introduction to this draft, he explains the meaning of his subtitle. Freud writes:

As the sexual union of horse and donkey produces two different hybrids, the mule [*Maulthier*] and the hinny [*Maulesel*], so the mixture of historical writing and fiction gives rise to different products which, under the common designation of "historical novel," sometimes want to be appreciated as history, sometimes as novel. For some of them deal with people and events that are historically familiar and whose characteristics they aim to reproduce faithfully. They derive their interest, in fact, from history, but their intent is that of the novel; they want to affect the emotions. Others among these literary creations function in quite the opposite way. They do not hesitate to invent persons and even events in order to describe the special character of a period, but first and foremost they aspire to historical truth despite the admitted fiction. Others even manage to a large extent in reconciling the demands of artistic creation with those of historical fidelity. How much fiction, contrary to the intentions of the historian, still creeps into his presentation, requires little further comment.

Freud goes on to say that he is "neither a historian nor an artist" and that his use of the title "historical novel" is intended in another (third) sense. His immediate purpose is "to gain knowledge of the person of Moses" and his more distant goal is "to contribute thereby to the solution of a problem, still current today, which can only be specified later on." Although Freud does not specify this problem here, he is referring to the problem of how to account for the distinctive character of the Jewish people (and their ability to survive). He concludes this short introduction as follows:

A character study requires reliable material as its basis, but nothing available concerning Moses can be called trustworthy. It is a tradition coming from one source, not confirmed by any other, fixed in writing only in a later period, in itself contradictory, revised several times and distorted under the influence of new tendencies, while closely interwoven with the religious and national myths of a people.

One would be entitled to curtail the attempt as hopeless, were it not that the grandeur of the figure outweighs its elusiveness and challenges us to renewed effort. Thus, one undertakes to treat each possibility in the text as a clue, and to fill the gap between one fragment and another according to the law, so to speak, of least resistance, that is – to give preference to the assumption that has the greatest probability. That which one can obtain by means of this technique can also be called a kind of "historical novel," since it has no proven reality, or only an unconfirmable one, for even the greatest probability does not necessarily correspond to the truth. Truth is often very improbable, and factual evidence can only in small measure be replaced by deductions and speculations.[23]

Freud decided to drop the subtitle "An Historical Novel," and he never published this Introduction. Shortly after he completed his draft, he wrote to Max Eitingon, "I am no good at historical novels; let us leave them to Thomas Mann" (*FM*, 18). There is no mention of "historical novels" in the published version of *The Man Moses and the Monotheistic Religion*, but Freud did *not* drop his references to "historical truth." The concept of historical truth which he distinguishes from material truth becomes especially important for Freud. (We have already cited Freud's reference to this distinction in his letter to Lou Andreas-Salomé.) In *The Man Moses and the Monotheistic Religion*, Freud reiterates this distinction: "We too believe that the pious solution contains the truth – but the *historical* truth and not the *material* truth" (23:129).[24]

One might think that by "historical truth" Freud means something like getting the historical facts straight – discovering who Moses really was and what really happened when Moses led the Israelites out of Egypt – the type of truth that an historian seeks to establish by an appeal to "objective evidence." But we will soon see that this is not what Freud means by "historical truth." Indeed, figuring out what Freud means by "historical truth" is complicated because he actually makes a tripartite distinction: eternal truth, historical truth, and material truth.

In order to understand these distinctions, we need to go back to what Freud says in the section entitled: "What is True in Religion." Throughout his *Moses* book (and indeed, throughout most of his life) Freud never concealed his militant atheism or his pride in being a member of the Jewish people. Freud is stubbornly and consistently Feuerbachian – at least insofar as his conviction that the gods (including the single omnipotent God of monotheism) are ultimately human creations – created in order to satisfy unconscious psychological needs of human beings. It is not God who created man, but man who created God. Furthermore, it was not God, but *the man* (*Der Mann*) Moses who created the Jewish people.

Freud begins the section, "What is True in Religion" with apparent sarcasm.

How enviable, to those of us who are poor in faith, do those enquirers seem who are convinced of the existence of a Supreme Being! To that great Spirit the world offers no problems, for he himself created all its institutions. How comprehensive, how exhaustive and how definitive are the doctrines of believers compared with the laborious, paltry and fragmentary attempts at explanation which are the most we are able to achieve! The divine Spirit, which is itself the ideal of ethical perfection, has planted in men the knowledge of that ideal and, at the same time, the urge to assimilate their own nature to it. They perceive directly what is higher and nobler and what is lower and more base. Their affective life is regulated in accordance with their distance from the ideal at any moment. When they approach to it – at their perihelion, as it were – they are brought high satisfaction; when, at their aphelion, they have become remote from it, the punishment is severe unpleasure. All of this is laid down so simply and so unshakably. We can only regret that certain experiences in life and observations in the world make it impossible for us to accept the premiss of the existence of such a Supreme Being. As though the world had not riddles enough, we are set the new problem of understanding how these other people have been able to acquire their belief in the Divine Being and whence that belief obtained its immense power, which overwhelms 'reason and science'. (23:122–3)

Although Freud is clearly distancing himself from the pious believer, it would be wrong to think that Freud is mocking or ridiculing the believer. His attitude is more akin to that other great contemporary Viennese thinker, Wittgenstein, when he declares at the end of his famous "Lecture on Ethics":

My whole tendency and I believe the tendency of all men who ever tried to write or talk Ethics or Religion was to run against the boundaries of language. This running against the walls of our cage is perfectly, absolutely hopeless. Ethics so far as it springs from the desire to say something about the ultimate meaning of life, the absolute good, the absolute valuable, can be no science. What it says does not add to our knowledge in any sense. *But it is a document of a tendency in the human mind which I personally cannot help respecting deeply and I would not for my life ridicule it.*[25]

Freud seeks to grasp what religion reveals about the development of human culture and what it tells us about the human psyche. In the passage immediately following the one above, Freud makes the claim which contains the sentence that has served as one of the epigraphs for this book. Here is the full context:

Let us return to the more modest problem which has occupied us hitherto. We wanted to explain the origin of the special character of the Jewish people, a character which is probably what has made their survival to the present day possible. We found that the man Moses impressed this character on them by giving them a religion which increased their self-esteem so much that they thought themselves superior to all other peoples. Thereafter they survived by keeping apart from others. Mixtures of blood interfered little with this, since what held them together was an ideal factor, the possession in common of certain intellectual and emotional wealth. The religion of Moses led to this result because (1) it allowed the people to take a share in the grandeur of a new idea of God, (2) it asserted that this people had been chosen by this great God and were destined to receive evidences of his special favour and (3) it forced upon the people an advance in intellectuality [*einen Fortschritt in der Geistigkeit*] which, important enough in itself, opened the way, in addition, to the appreciation of intellectual work [*der intellektuellen Arbeit*] and to further renunciations of instinct. (23:123)[26]

With this background we can now turn directly to clarifying the meaning and significance of the tripartite distinction: eternal truth, historical truth, and material truth. Pious believers do have an "explanation" for the grandeur of their belief in one God of the universe. "They say that the idea of a single god produced such an overwhelming effect on men because it is a portion of the eternal *truth* which, long concealed, came to light at last and was then bound to carry everyone along with it" (23:129). Eternal truth then is the truth of the revelation of God himself. Freud says "[w]e too would like to accept this solution" but are prevented from doing so because of serious doubts. It is not just that Freud doubts the existence of a Supreme Being, but he thinks that "[t]he pious argument rests on an optimistic and idealistic premiss." It assumes that "the human mind shows [a] special inclination for recognizing the truth. We have rather found, on the contrary, that our intellect very easily goes astray without any warning, and that nothing is more easily believed by us than what, without reference to the truth, comes to meet our wishful illusions" (23:129).[27] But, nevertheless, Freud affirms: "We too believe that the pious solution contains the truth – but the *historical* truth and not the *material* truth."

Freud's reasoning here illustrates his master strategy as a practitioner of the hermeneutics of suspicion. The "pious argument" does contain "the truth" – but it distorts this truth. It is not the revelation of a supernatural eternal truth. Rather there is "a certain distortion" (*eine gewisse Entstellung*) in this "pious solution."

What then is the "historical truth" that lies hidden and distorted in the "pious solution"? Freud states it succinctly: "That is to say, we do not believe that there is a single great god to-day, but that in primaeval times there was a single person who was bound to appear huge at that time and who afterwards returned in men's memory elevated to divinity" (23:129). Explaining this hypothesis more fully (and explicating the analogy between the psychological development of an individual neurosis and a religious tradition), Freud writes:

We had assumed that the religion of Moses was to begin with rejected and half-forgotten and afterwards broke through as a tradition. We are now assuming that this process was being repeated then for the second time. When Moses brought the people the idea of a single god, it was not a novelty but signified the revival of an experience in the primaeval ages of the human family which had long vanished from men's conscious memory. But it had been so important and had produced or paved the way for such deeply penetrating changes in men's life that we cannot avoid believing that it had left behind it in the human mind some permanent traces, which can be compared to a tradition.

We have learnt from the psycho-analyses of individuals that their earliest impressions, received at a time when the child was scarcely yet capable of speaking, produce at some time or another effects of a compulsive character without themselves being consciously remembered. We believe we have a right to make the same assumption about the earliest experiences of the whole of humanity. One of the effects would be the emergence of the idea of a single great god – an idea which must be recognized as a completely justified memory, though, it is true, one that has been distorted. An idea such as this has a compulsive character: it *must* be believed. To the extent to which it is distorted, it may be described as a *delusion*; in so far as it brings a return of the past, it must be called the *truth*. (23:129–30)

The historical truth then is truth that "brings a return of the past." The specific historical truth that he is speaking about is the murder of the primal father. When Freud contrasts "historical truth" with "material truth," he wants to distinguish the former from what is manifest and literal. Religious claims qua *religious* are "materially" false. They purport to make claims about the world (or what is beyond the world), but they are literally false. Nevertheless, although materially or literally false, we should not simply dismiss these claims. We must seek to decipher them, to discover what is hidden and distorted in these materially false claims, to discover the kernel of truth that they contain. In short, we must *reverse* the process of transformation that conceals the historical truth. What psychoanalysis enables us to discover is this historical truth, and the deep psychological truth that these materially false claims distort.

Freud himself showed little interest in competing philosophic theories of truth, although his dominant orientation is to favor a version of what philosophers call "realism" – the conviction that there is a "fact of the matter," an objective truth to be known, even though we may never know it with finality or certainty. But it is worth reflecting on the oddities of his understanding of "historical truth." For this is a conception of truth no "ordinary historian" would accept. Suppose we ask, as a historian, anthropologist, or ethnologist might: is there solid (or even plausible) evidence that warrants the claim that there really were primitive hordes ruled by despotic fathers – fathers who were murdered and devoured by their sons? There are few serious scholars (if any) who would accept Freud's claim that this is the "historical truth." On the contrary, it has more of the character of a myth – one invented by Freud to "explain" the origin of religion and morality. When Freud wrote his *Moses* book, he was keenly aware of the sharp criticisms of his claims about the origins of "totemic religion," but he was unmoved by them. He did not hesitate to indicate his radical departure from the unanimity of scholarly opinion.

I have repeatedly met with violent reproaches for not having altered my opinions in later editions of my book [*Totem and Taboo*] in spite of the fact that more recent ethnologists have unanimously rejected Robertson Smith's hypotheses and have in part brought forward other, totally divergent theories. I may say in reply that these ostensible advances are well known to me. But I have not been convinced either of the correctness of these innovations or of Robertson Smith's errors. A denial is not a refutation, an innovation is not necessarily an advance. Above all, however, I am not an ethnologist but a psycho-analyst. I had a right to take out of ethnological literature what I might need for the work of analysis. The writings of Robertson Smith – a man of genius – have given me valuable points of contact with the psychological material of analysis and indications for its employment. I have never found myself on common ground with his opponents. (23:131–2)

It is certainly true that a "denial is not a refutation, an innovation is not necessarily an advance," but Freud does not give any *reasons* why he so "firmly" holds to his original construction, why he has "not been convinced either of the correctness of these innovations or of Robertson Smith's errors." It is not a good reason to declare that one is a psychoanalyst, since what is presumably at issue is an empirical hypothesis based on ethnological research. It begins to look as if Freud's conviction about the historical truth of his totem theory is impervious to any rational criticism; it is not even clear what Freud would consider to be a refutation of his theory about the totemic origins of religion and morality. Freud seems to be blind to the fact that the criticism he makes of the doctrine "*credo quia absurdum*" – a "claim to truth against which logical objections remain powerless" (23:85) – is just as applicable to his notion of "historical truth." Freud, nevertheless, was convinced that he had discovered the "historical truth" that enabled him to penetrate to what lay behind the Jewish religious tradition – the murder of the primal father.

There is another striking peculiarity about this understanding of "historical truth." Despite appearances to the contrary, the primary evidence for it is not some real discovery that Freud has made about what happened in the *past*. It is rather his *present* psychoanalytic under-standing of the unconscious dynamics of individuals that provides Freud with evidence that he has discovered the "historical truth." There is a *double* temporal perspective that runs throughout the *Moses* study. The rhetorical structure of the book, and Freud's historical narrative about the Egyptian origins of Moses, lead us to think that Freud is giving us an account of the character of the Jewish people by appealing to what happened in the past. But this explanatory narrative is itself constructed primarily on the basis of our *present* psychoanalytic understanding of the dynamics of the human psyche. In the 1935 Postscript to his "Autobio-graphical Study," Freud makes a very revealing statement about the "logic" of his reasoning concerning the origins of religion and morality. (This was written after he completed his 1934 draft of the *Moses* book but before he had published his findings.)

My interest, after making a lifelong *détour* through the natural sciences, medi-cine and psychotherapy, returned to the cultural problems which had fas-cinated me long before, when I was a youth scarcely old enough for thinking. At the very climax of my psycho-analytic work, in 1912, I had already attempted in *Totem and Taboo* to make use of the newly discovered findings of analysis in order to investigate the origins of religion and morality. I now carried this work a stage further in two later essays, *The Future of an Illusion* . . . and *Civilization and its Discontents* . . . I perceived ever more clearly that the events of human history, the interactions between human nature, cultural development and the precipi-tates of primaeval experiences (the most prominent example of which is religion) *are no more than a reflection of the dynamic conflicts between the ego, the id and the super-ego, which psycho-analysis studies in the individual – are the very same processes repeated upon a wider stage.* (20:72, emphasis added)

This passage is important but not simply because it reiterates what Freud tells us over and over again – that the starting point and basis for his speculation about the history of culture (especially religion) is grounded in the psychoanalytic study of individuals. Rather, it enables us to understand more clearly the unstable double temporal perspective of his analysis of religious phenomena. It looks as if Freud seeks to

explain what is distinctive about religious traditions by an appeal to
what happened in the past. But the character of this "historical truth" is
itself based on our current psychoanalytic understanding of the dynamics of the human psyche. There is a reversal of the presumed explanatory force of the appeal to "origins." Freud is not really explaining the
historical truth of the Jewish religious tradition by an appeal to "events"
which presumably occurred in a shadowy historical past. Rather he is
projecting what allegedly happened in the past – "the historical truth" –
on the basis of our understanding of the dynamical conflicts of the
human psyche. This becomes evident when we realize that even if we
grant the "material truth" of the claims that Freud makes about the past
– from the origin of totemic religions through the murder of Moses, this
would not explain what Freud seeks to explain, the character of the
Jewish people, unless it is *presupposed* that these events conform to the
formulaic schema of "early trauma – defence – latency – outbreak of
neurosis – partial return of the repressed." The presupposition that such
a pattern did occur is not based on any discoveries about the historical
past. On the contrary, Freud's interpretation of past events is itself based
upon this formulaic pattern. It is the grid by which he reads the
psychological prehistory of religion and morality. To put the point in a
slightly paradoxical manner, Freud does not explain the character of the
Jewish religious tradition by an appeal to the "historical truth." He
explains the "historical truth" of this tradition by an appeal to our
present psychoanalytic understanding of the dynamics of the human
psyche.[28]

Freud's emphatic claim that "the precipitates of primaeval experiences . . . are no more than a reflection of the dynamic conflicts between
the ego, the id and the super-ego" is important for another reason. It
bears on the fundamental question of how one is to read and interpret
what Freud is actually doing in *The Man Moses and the Monotheistic Religion*.
On the *manifest* level, this is a book about the Egyptian origins of Jewish
monotheism and the historical vicissitudes of the Mosaic ideals in
shaping the character of the Jewish people. But we cannot ignore the
latent content of Freud's narrative.[29] I am not referring to Freud's own
psyche, but to what is latent in his text – in what he is saying. Freud's
remarks about the "reflections of the dynamic conflicts between the ego,
the id and the super-ego" should *not* be read in a flat reductionistic
manner (as they so frequently have been read). Throughout I have been
arguing that we must be alert to the ways in which Freud is basing his
cultural analyses on his clinical observation of individuals, and we must

also be sensitive to the subtle ways in which Freud struggles to do justice to what is distinctive about these cultural processes. Indeed, there is something misleading in the very idea of "applied psychoanalysis" – at least, insofar as it may suggest a one-way route of application. "Applied psychoanalysis" may mislead us into thinking that first we develop the concepts required for the psychoanalysis of neurotic individuals and then we apply them in a straightforward manner to group and cultural phenomena. But Freud is much more dialectical and subtle in what he actually does. His cultural analyses in *Totem and Taboo*, *Civilization and its Discontents*, and *The Man Moses and the Monotheistic Religion* supplement, modify, and *deepen* our understanding of the dynamic conflicts of the ego, the id, and the super-ego in *individuals*. Our understanding of these dynamic conflicts in individuals is enhanced by the study of culture. There is also something misleading about the distinction that Freud himself reiterates – the distinction between the individual and the group. This is, at best, a (tentative) heuristic distinction that requires modification. The dynamic conflicts that play themselves out in religion are not mere superstructures or epiphenomena. They are constitutive of the very psychic fabric of "individuals" who are shaped by these "cultural" phenomena. Consequently, we should read *The Man Moses and the Monotheistic Religion* as contributing to a further understanding of the dynamic conflicts of id, ego, and super-ego. The genesis of morality, the psychic formation of conscience, the achievement of civilization, and *Der Fortschritt in der Geistigkeit* all require the renunciation of instinct. The problem – the central paradox – that lies at the core of Freud's cultural writings is that the achievements of civilization and *Geistigkeit* presuppose and exacerbate a sense of guilt. Furthermore, Freud's *Moses* is also a book about the problem of conscience, of authority, of our psychological ambivalence toward authority, and of the internalization of authority. The "great man" Moses is the great father figure – the figure of authority. He symbolizes a strict and demanding super-ego – one that has exacerbated the sense of guilt in the Jewish religious tradition. Fathers and father figures are not only loved, revered, and honored. They are also feared and hated. Sons must rebel against their fathers in order to resolve their Oedipal conflicts. This also includes rebelling against the authority figure of Moses himself. We should not forget that at the very beginning of his study, Freud declares: "A hero is someone who has had the courage to rebel against his father and has in the end victoriously overcome him" (23:12). In *The Man Moses and the Monotheistic Religion* we witness Freud's own rebellion against Moses and his attempt to overcome him. The authority of Moses and his monotheistic religion is overthrown and displaced with the new authority of reason manifested in the science of psychoanalysis.

Freud is certainly not a cultural optimist. He is suspicious of all forms of utopianism. But it is misleading to characterize him as a pessimist. As a cultural diagnostician, he is a *realist* who claims that there is no escape from the psychic conflicts that result from the renunciation of instincts and the guilt that this renunciation engenders. Freud is also painfully aware that the triumph of monotheism in the course of Jewish history and *Der Fortschritt in der Geistigkeit* achieved by this strict, demanding form of monotheism has meant that the Jewish people have "taken a tragic load of guilt on themselves" and "have been made to pay heavy penance for it" (23:136).

CHAPTER 3

Anti-Semitism, Christianity, and Judaism

ANTI-SEMITISM AND CHRISTIANITY

I want to consider two other interrelated aspects of the *Moses* book: Freud's reflections on anti-Semitism and Christianity. Both of these topics are relevant for completing our analysis of Freud's concern with the distinctive character of the Jewish people. They will also enable us to understand a theme which plays an increasing role in Freud's mature thinking about the development of civilization – the extent to which this development is itself based upon a sense of guilt – a sense of guilt that results from the repression and the renunciation of instincts. According to Freud, this sense of guilt, especially strong among the Jewish people, was kept alive by the Prophets. The insatiable need to satisfy it eventually led to the imposition of "more and more new instinctual renunciations." And these resulted in "ethical heights which had remained inaccessible to the other peoples of antiquity" (23:134).

It would be a mistake to think that Freud's discussions of anti-Semitism and Christianity are somehow afterthoughts to Freud's analysis of Mosaic monotheism. On the contrary, it is not an exaggeration to say that Freud's intense concern with anti-Semitism – especially Christian anti-Semitism – set the problematic that he wanted to address in his *Moses* book. Let us recall that in September, 1934 Freud wrote to Arnold Zweig: "Faced with the new persecutions, one asks oneself again how the Jews have come to be what they are and why they have attracted this undying hatred" (*SFAZ*, 91). Note the way in which Freud phrases this question. He does not ask what is it that characterizes the anti-Semite, but rather, what is it about the Jews that attracts this *undying* hatred.

Freud does not seek to give a complete account of anti-Semitism. "A phenomenon of such intensity and permanence as the people's hatred of the Jews must of course have more than one ground" (23:90). He considers some of the manifest reasons for this hatred: that the Jews are an "alien" people; that they have been minorities and have served as scapegoats because "the communal feeling of groups requires, in order to complete it, hostility towards some extraneous minority" (23:90). The very differences of the Jewish people from their host populations have been a source of hostility. "[I]ntolerance of groups is often, strangely enough, exhibited more strongly against small differences than against fundamental ones" (23:91). The fact that the Jews have defied all oppression, that they have stubbornly resisted conversion and assimilation, and "that the most cruel persecutions have not succeeded in exterminating them" has also provoked hatred of them. But these factors have been cited by many others – and none of them are based upon any special psychoanalytic insight. Psychoanalysis can make a special contribution to understanding anti-Semitism by focusing attention on the unconscious motives for hatred – deeper motives which are "rooted in the remotest ages." Freud ventures "to assert that jealousy of the people which declared itself the first-born, favourite child of God the Father, has not yet been surmounted among other peoples even today: it is as though they had thought there was truth in the claim" (23:91). He also indicates that the custom of circumcision "has made a disagreeable, uncanny impression [*unheimlichen Eindruck*], which is to be explained, no doubt, by its recalling the dreaded castration and along with it a portion of the primaeval past which is gladly forgotten" (23:91). One of the most curious reasons that Freud gives for anti-Semitism is the following:

[W]e must not forget that all those peoples who excel to-day in their hatred of Jews became Christians only in late historic times, often driven to it by bloody coercion. It might be said that they are all 'misbaptized'. They have been left, under a thin veneer of Christianity, what their ancestors were, who worshipped a barbarous polytheism. They have not got over a grudge against the new religion which was imposed on them; but they have displaced the grudge on to the source from which Christianity reached them. The fact that the Gospels tell a story which is set among Jews, and in fact deals only with Jews, has made this displacement easy for them. Their hatred of Jews is at bottom a hatred of Christians, and we need not be surprised that in the German National-Socialist revolution this intimate relation between the two monotheist religions finds such a clear expression in the hostile treatment of both of them. (23:91–2)

This means that anti-Semitism when it is unmasked is "at bottom" a hatred of Christians by "misbaptized" Christians! What is especially interesting about this "latest motive" is what it tells us about how Freud understands the relation of Christianity to Judaism. Freud, as we have emphasized, deeply admires the purity of the monotheism professed by

Moses and the Jewish Prophets – the monotheism that condemns all forms of idolatry and "barbarous polytheism." Freud links strict monotheism with the adherence to the highest ethical ideals – living a life of truth and justice. Although Freud does not elaborate the point here, his analysis also helps to make sense of the Nazi attraction to the revival of polytheistic mythology as an expression of its hostility toward "the two monotheist religions."[1]

Freud, as we have seen, stresses the distinction between the pure monotheism of Judaism with its prohibition against graven images from the "regression" to the polytheistic backsliding that he finds in Christianity. But this is not "the whole story." From our discussion of the "historical truth" of religion we have learned that the most important element in the origin of religion is the deep psychological ambivalence toward, and eventual murder of, the primeval father – a murder that is repeated in the murder of Moses. But this is also important for understanding Christianity and Christian anti-Semitism. "It is plausible to conjecture that remorse for the murder of Moses provided the stimulus for the wishful phantasy of the Messiah, who was to return and lead his people to redemption and the promised world-dominion" (23:89).

If Moses was this first Messiah, Christ became his substitute and successor, and Paul could exclaim to the peoples with some historical justification: 'Look! the Messiah has really come: he has been murdered before your eyes!' Then, too, there is a piece of historical truth in Christ's resurrection, for he was the resurrected Moses and behind him the returned primal father of the primitive horde, transfigured and, as the son, put in place of the father. (23:89–90)

There is a Christian theological tradition that claims that the biblical narrative of Moses anticipates the coming of Christ, the Messiah. But Freud is not engaging in theological speculation. He is seeking to decipher the distortion that lies hidden in this theological tradition – what he calls the "historical truth in Christ's resurrection." And here the repetitive pattern that Freud claims to have discovered is underscored: murder of the primal father, murder of Moses, murder of Christ. The memory-traces of this "transfigured" event persist, and it is evoked by the repetition of the trauma of the primal murder. The trauma is both forgotten (repressed) and remembered (re-lived).

The poor Jewish people, who with their habitual stubbornness continued to disavow the father's murder, atoned heavily for it in the course of time. They were constantly met with the reproach 'You killed our God!' And this reproach is true, if it is correctly translated. If it is brought into relation with the history of religions, it runs: 'You will not *admit* that you murdered God (the primal picture of God, the primal father, and his later reincarnations).' There should be an addition declaring: 'We did the same thing, to be sure, but we have *admitted* it and since then we have been absolved.' (23:90)

But the Jews could never admit that they had murdered their father, Moses. And despite the "ethical heights" of their demanding mono-theism, they have paid a heavy psychological price for this refusal. Christians (albeit in a distorted manner) do admit that they have murdered their God. This admission is the basis of their "son-religion," and a source of deep hostility against the Jews.

There was no place in the framework of the religion of Moses for a direct expression of the murderous hatred of the father. All that could come to light was a mighty reaction against it – a sense of guilt on account of that hostility, a bad conscience for having sinned against God and for not ceasing to sin. This sense of guilt . . . was uninterruptedly kept awake by the Prophets, and . . . soon formed an essential part of the religious system. (23:134)

We must emphasize again that Freud is analyzing Jewish and Chris-tian monotheism from a psychoanalytic perspective. Freud never wa-vers in his own atheism and in believing that psychoanalysis entails atheism. When he speaks about the "regression" that takes place with the coming of Christianity, and the sense in which Christianity can also be seen as a "forward step," when he declares that Judaism became a "fossil," he is not making religious or theological claims about the superiority of one form of monotheism over another. As a psycho-analyst, his attention is directed to the psychological needs and wishes that a given form of religion satisfies and to discovering its psychic costs. The Jewish people suffered from a "growing sense of guilt" which resulted from the remorse of repeating the murder of the primal father. But the Jews could not admit that they had murdered their father. And here we can see the contribution of the Roman Jew, Saul of Tarsus – Paul.

It appears as though a growing sense of guilt had taken hold of the Jewish people, or perhaps of the whole civilized world of the time, as a precursor to the return of the repressed material. Till at last one of these Jewish people found, in justifying a politico-religious agitator, the occasion for detaching a new – the Christian – religion from Judaism. Paul, a Roman Jew from Tarsus, seized upon this sense of guilt and traced it back correctly to its original source. He called this the 'original sin'; it was a crime against God and could only be atoned for by death. With the original sin death came into the world. In fact this crime deserving death had been the murder of the primal father who was later deified. But the murder was not remembered: instead of it there was a phantasy of its atonement, and for that reason this phantasy could be hailed as a message of redemption (*evangelium*). A son of God had allowed himself to be killed without guilt and had thus taken on himself the guilt of all men. It had to be a son, since it had been the murder of a father. It is probable that traditions from oriental and Greek mysteries had had an influence on the phantasy of redemption. What was essential in it seems to have been Paul's own contribution. In the most proper sense he was a man of an innately religious disposition: the dark traces of the past lurked in his mind, ready to break through into its more conscious regions. (23:86–7)

Freud leaves no doubt about his psychoanalytic diagnosis of Paul's Christianity when he immediately adds: "That the redeemer had sacrificed himself without guilt was evidently a tendentious distortion [*tendenziose Entstellung*], which offered difficulties to logical understanding" (23:87).

Even though it was a Jew, Saul of Tarsus, who founded the new religion of Christianity, there is a major psychological difference between Judaism and Christianity. With Christianity there is "the delusional disguise of the glad tidings" (23:135). There is redemption by the sacrifice of the son of God.

And the intermediate step between the delusion and the historical truth was provided by the assurance that the victim of the sacrifice had been God's son. With the strength which it derived from the source of historical truth, this new faith overthrew every obstacle. The blissful sense of being chosen was replaced by the liberating sense of redemption . . . The unnamable crime was replaced by the hypothesis of what must be described as a shadowy 'original sin'. (23:135)

Consequently, "[o]riginal sin and redemption by the sacrifice of a victim became the foundation stones of the new religion founded by Paul" (23:135). Christian doctrine "burst the framework of Judaism." Subsequently, "it took up components from many other sources, renounced a number of characteristics of pure monotheism and adapted itself in many details to the rituals of the other Mediterranean peoples. It was as though Egypt was taking vengeance once more on the heirs of Akhenaten" (23:136).

It is worth noticing how the new religion dealt with the ancient ambivalence in the relation to the father. Its main content was, it is true, reconciliation with God the Father, atonement for the crime committed against him; but the other side of the emotional relation showed itself in the fact that the son, who had taken the atonement on himself, became a god himself beside the father and, actually, in the place of the father. Christianity, having arisen out of a father-religion, became a son-religion. It has not escaped the fate of having to get rid of the father. (23:136)

Freud concludes his sketch of "The Historical Development" of religion by reiterating the reproach that Christians have brought against the Jews. "You have murdered our God!" "In full, this reproach would run as follows: '[The Jews] will not accept it as true that they murdered God, whereas we admit and have been cleansed of that guilt'" (23:136).

We see here the complexities of Freud's understanding of the relation between Judaism and Christianity. On the one hand, Freud repeats a dominant theme of his *Moses* book, that Christianity is a regression from the pure Mosaic monotheism – a regression that repeats what happened in Egypt when the priests of Amun sought their revenge against the monotheistic religion of Akhenaten. And it is this revenge that helps to account for Christian anti-Semitism. But on the other hand, Christianity represents a "forward step," at least in so far as it is a religion that is based upon the admission and acknowledgment of the murder of God, the Father. But this admission is achieved by distortion – blaming the murder on the Jews. Freud does not, however, answer the question why the Jewish people refused to take this "forward step." "A special enquiry would be called for to discover why it has been impossible for the Jews to join in this forward step which was implied, in spite of all its distortions, by the admission of having murdered God. In a certain sense they have in that way taken a tragic load of guilt on themselves; they have been made to pay heavy penance for it" (23:136). But despite this "tragic load of guilt," Freud clearly identifies with the Mosaic ideal which stubbornly refuses to regress back into any form of "barbaric polytheism."

THE DENOUEMENT: "WHAT IS THERE LEFT TO YOU THAT IS JEWISH?"

On June 4, 1938, less than three months after the Nazis marched into Vienna, Freud was finally allowed to leave Vienna. He was eighty-two years old, suffering from the debilitating effects of a painful cancer, and anticipating his own death, but he wanted to "die in freedom."[2] Accompanied by his daughter, Anna, he traveled to England, stopping overnight in Paris where he stayed with Marie Bonaparte, his loyal friend who had helped to secure his freedom. Although Freud had decided not to publish Part III of his *Moses* book while he was still living in Vienna, he was now eager to complete the final draft. Freud wanted his book to be published while he was still alive. Two weeks after his arrival in London, he noted in his Chronik, "Moses III started again." And on July 17, he announced to his brother, Alexander, "Have just written down the last sentence of my Moses III." By the time Freud finished the book there were wild rumors about what it contained, and all sorts of appeals for him not to publish it. But Freud was determined to have it published (and translated into English) just as he had written it.[3] He resisted even the "slight suggestions" for revision made by his American publisher. As Peter Gay notes, he "professed to believe that what others called his obstinacy or arrogance was really a sign of modesty. He was not influential enough, he argued, to disturb the faith of a single believing Jew."[4] In one of his disclaimers, he wrote:

No one who seeks consolation in the holy Bible or in the prayers of the synagogue is in danger of loosing [sic] his faith by my preachings. I even think he will not come to learn, whatever it is I believe and defend in my books. Faith cannot be shaken by such means. I do not write for the people or the mass of believers. I just produce scientific stuff for the interest of a minority which has no faith to loose [sic].[5]

Freud's assertions in this letter are consistent with what he says in *The Man Moses and the Monotheistic Religion* and in his other writings dealing with religious faith. One of the main points of the analogy that Freud draws between religious belief and obsessional neurosis is to underscore the compulsive power of religious belief – including Judaism. We must not underestimate this power which can overwhelm what we learn from science (in particular, the science of psychoanalysis).

Freud's own repetitions are always instructive and revealing. He cites the famous "*credo quia absurdum*" twice. And each time he is making a similar point about the "peculiar force" [*besonderer Macht*] of religious faith.

It is worth specially stressing the fact that each portion which returns from oblivion asserts itself with peculiar force, exercises an incomparably powerful influence on people in the mass, and raises an irresistible claim to truth against which logical objections remain powerless: a kind of '*credo quia absurdum*'. This remarkable feature can only be understood on the pattern of the delusions of psychotics. (23:85)

And again:

Thus we are faced by the phenomenon that in the course of the development of humanity sensuality [*Sinnlichkeit*] is gradually overpowered by intellectuality [*Geistigkeit*] and that men feel proud and exalted by every such advance [*Fortschritt*]. But we are unable to say why this should be so. It further happens later on that intellectuality itself is overpowered by the very puzzling emotional phenomenon of faith. Here we have the celebrated '*credo quia absurdum*' . . . (23:118)

When we draw out the logical consequences of Freud's assertions, we can see that he is cautioning us about optimistic secularization and modernization theories that underestimate the compulsive power of religious belief. Freud would not be shocked or surprised by the recent resurgence of religious fundamentalism that has erupted throughout the world. For this phenomenon itself is a "return of the repressed." There is also a darker consequence that follows from what Freud says. It is utopian to think that rational arguments are sufficient to put an end to anti-Semitism – especially Christian anti-Semitism – insofar as religious anti-Semitism is itself grounded in the compulsive force of religious faith. This, of course, does not in any way diminish the responsibility of the intellectual to seek to understand the psychological dynamics of religious prejudice – and to oppose it. For Freud, in his more rationalistic modes, also maintained that after many rebuffs, the soft voice of intellect and reason will eventually triumph. As he declared in *The Future of an Illusion*: "This is one of the few points on which one may be optimistic about the future of mankind" (21:53).

The segment of Part III that Freud initially shared with his psychoanalytic colleagues was "*Der Fortschritt in der Geistigkeit*." The International Psychoanalytical Congress was scheduled to meet in Paris in August, 1938. Freud was too old and feeble to travel to Paris; but he asked Anna to read this section on his behalf to the Congress. This is the brief section where Freud presents a summary of his analysis of the cultural significance of the Mosaic monotheistic religion and its profound effect on the character of the Jewish people. It is here that Freud insists that there is no precept of greater importance in the Mosaic religion than "the prohibition against making an image of God – the compulsion to worship a God whom one cannot see" (23:112–3). It is here too that Freud tells the story about the founding of "the first Torah school" by Rabbi Jochanan ben Zakkai, a story that serves as a parable about what enabled the Jewish people to survive through the long history of their persecutions. "From that time on, the Holy Writ and intellectual concern with it were what held the scattered people together" (23:115). Why did Freud select this section to be read before the Paris International Psychoanalytic Congress? After all, it barely contains any reference or contribution to psychoanalysis. Let me suggest that Freud intended to leave a testament to his fellow psychoanalysts – to remind them of what he passionately believed – that psychoanalysis represented a further development in *Der Fortschritt in der Geistigkeit*. Freud, the proud godless Jew, conceived of his own discovery of psychoanalysis as continuous with the tradition introduced by "the great man" Moses, whose legacy had decisively influenced the character of the Jewish people.

We might also ask, as Freud himself does, why is it that *Der Fortschritt in der Geistigkeit*, a set-back in sensuality [*Sinnlichkeit*], "should raise the self-regard both of an individual and of a people" (23:116)? Freud draws upon his analysis of the renunciation of instinct and the development of the super-ego in order to answer this question. It is the id that "gives rise to an instinctual demand of an erotic or aggressive nature." And it is the ego "which has the apparatus of thought and the muscular apparatus at its disposal" that tries to satisfy this instinctual demand. The ego may abstain from satisfying these instinctual demands because of "external obstacles." It is even more important when the ego abstains from doing the bidding of the id because of "internal" reasons – when it is obedient to the super-ego, the agency "constructed in the ego which confronts the rest of the ego in an observing, criticizing and prohibiting sense . . . Thenceforward the ego, before putting to work the instinctual satisfactions demanded by the id, has to take into account not merely the dangers of the external world but also the objections of the super-ego, and it will have all the more grounds for abstaining from satisfying the instinct" (23:116). But such renunciation is not only unpleasurable. Obedience to the super-ego has a different "economic effect." "In addition to the inevitable unpleasurable consequences it also brings the ego a yield of pleasure – a substitute satisfaction, as it were. The ego feels elevated; it is proud of the instinctual renunciation, as though it were a valuable achievement" (23:117).

It is typical of Freud to return to the psychological dynamics of the individual in order to shed light on the analogy that he wants to draw with the history of the Jewish people. "What help does this explanation of the satisfaction arising from instinctual renunciation give towards understanding the processes that we want to study – the elevation of self-regard when there are advances in intellectuality [*bei Fortschritten der Geistigkeit*]" (23:117)? After pointing out some of the disanalogies between the individual and the group, he nevertheless tells us:

The religion which began with the prohibition against making an image of God develops more and more in the course of centuries into a religion of instinctual renunciations. It is not that it would demand sexual *abstinence*; it is content with a marked restriction of sexual freedom. God, however, becomes entirely removed from sexuality and elevated into the ideal of ethical perfection. But ethics is a limitation of instinct. (23:118)

Here too Freud emphasizes the role of the Prophets in holding up before the Jewish people the ethical demands of Mosaic monotheism.

The Prophets are never tired of asseverating that God requires nothing other from his people than a just and virtuous conduct of life – that is, abstention from every instinctual satisfaction which is still condemned as vicious by our morality to-day as well. And even the demand for belief in him seems to take a second place in comparison with the seriousness of these ethical requirements. In this way instinctual renunciation seems to play a prominent part in the religion, even if it did not stand out in it from the first. (23:118–9)

We can now finally return to the thesis that I announced at the beginning of this inquiry: that the question that Freud raised in the preface to the Hebrew translation of *Totem and Taboo* is answered in *The Man Moses and the Monotheistic Religion*. Let us recall Freud's own words:

No reader of [the Hebrew version of] this book will find it easy to put himself in the emotional position of an author who is ignorant of the language of holy writ, who is completely estranged from the religion of his fathers – as well as from every other religion – and who cannot take a share in nationalist ideals, but who has yet never repudiated his people, who feels that he is in his essential nature a Jew and who has no desire to alter that nature. If the question were put to him: 'Since you have abandoned all these common characteristics of your countrymen, what is there left to you that is Jewish?' he would reply: 'A very great deal, and probably its very essence.' He could not now express that essence clearly in words; but some day, no doubt, it will become accessible to the scientific mind. (13:xv)

It is in *The Man Moses and the Monotheistic Religion* that Freud attempted "to express that essence clearly in words" the essence that Freud epitomizes in the phrase *"Der Fortschritt in der Geistigkeit."*[6] This is the enduring legacy of Mosaic monotheism – a legacy which Freud believed held the Jewish people together, and enabled the Jews to survive through centuries of persecution. It is a legacy that is at once intellectual, spiritual, and ethical; a legacy which outlasts the *religious* teachings of Judaism; a legacy with which Freud proudly identifies.

It would be an exaggeration and a falsification of Freud's views to suggest that the Mosaic monotheistic tradition was exclusively responsible for *Der Fortschritt in der Geistigkeit*. Such a claim would contradict Freud's basic conviction that mono-causal accounts are never sufficient to explain such complex cultural phenomena. Positively stated, there are various psychological, historical, and cultural phenomena that have contributed to the type of intellectual and spiritual advancement that Freud singles out as so important in the development of civilization. To acknowledge this is not in any way to diminish the significance of the contribution of the Jewish tradition to this "advance" and "progress" or Freud's pride in identifying himself with this tradition.

My primary aim in this book has been to show that a careful reading of *The Man Moses and the Monotheistic Religion* provides an answer to the specific question that Freud put to himself in the Hebrew preface to *Totem and Taboo*. But there are many other questions concerning Freud's Jewish identity and its significance for understanding psychoanalysis; and there is now an enormous secondary body of literature dealing with these issues.[7] We must distinguish carefully between several quite different issues which are frequently combined in a confusing manner. There are questions concerning Freud's upbringing, his relation with his Jewish father and mother, his early Hebrew education, whether he knew more Hebrew and Yiddish than he frequently professed to know, and whether consciously or unconsciously Freud was influenced by Jewish sources in his psychoanalytic writings (and which sources they may have been). I do not want to slight the importance of these questions and the controversies that they have generated. Judicious answers to them can certainly facilitate understanding of Freud the man and his work.

In reading this extensive secondary literature, one receives the impression that the issue which most intrigues his commentators, and which has called forth the most heated and polemical controversies, is whether and in what way psychoanalysis is a "Jewish science." It is not difficult to understand why this issue has been such an emotional one – especially because this is the very accusation brought against psychoanalysis by anti-Semites. (I will address the issue of what Freud *believed* in my final chapter, my "dialogue" with Yerushalmi.)

The commentator who has most vehemently argued that there is no basis whatsoever for claiming that psychoanalysis is a Jewish science or that Freud ever even entertained this belief is his distinguished biographer, Peter Gay. Despite Gay's comprehensive command of all aspects of Freud's life and work, I think that his several attempts to put the issue to rest actually distort and obscure some basic questions.[8] Gay, who is also an outstanding historian of the Enlightenment seeks (correctly, in my opinion) to show that Freud exemplifies this great Enlightenment tradition in his commitment to reason, truth, and universal science. Furthermore, Freud would be scandalized by the suggestion that there is anything intrinsically Jewish (and therefore parochial) about the discipline of psychoanalysis that he founded. But Gay's militancy in defending this thesis leads him, at times, to neglect other important questions. Gay seems to think that to acknowledge that Freud was passionately concerned with understanding the essential character of the Jewish people and his own Jewishness would compromise the scientific status of psychoanalysis. Although I am sympathetic with Gay insofar as he seeks to show the deep sense in which Freud is an *Aufklärer*, I also think that Gay is at his weakest in dealing with the question that obsesses Freud: "what is there left to you that is Jewish?" The most important issues here are not only biographical, they are conceptual. I strongly believe that there is something fundamentally wrong with the tacit dichotomy – the binary opposition – that is frequently presupposed in these controversies: the dichotomy between being a Jew (and taking one's Jewish heritage seriously) and being an *Aufklärer* (committed to the Enlightenment ideals of universal science and rational critique). Freud was *both*, and he was proud of being both – a Jew and an *Aufklärer*. The Freud who emphatically affirmed himself as a Jew, and did this with increasing forcefulness during the period of the rise of the Nazis, is the same Freud who also declared: "[t]he voice of the intellect is a soft one, but it does not rest till it has gained a hearing. Finally, after a countless succession of rebuffs, it succeeds" (21:53).

What distinguishes Freud from so many of his contemporary German-Jewish and Austrian-Jewish colleagues is that he never hesitated in identifying himself as a Jew and as a champion of unprejudiced science. In this respect, Freud is the very *antithesis* of a "self-hating Jew." Furthermore, the most basic argument of *The Man Moses and the Monotheistic Religion* is that the essential and enduring achievement of the vexed legacy of Moses has been its contribution to the intellectual tradition that is also represented by Enlightenment *ideals*. Freud was, to use Kwame Anthony Appiah's very apt term, a "rooted cosmopolitan."[9] Although he distanced himself from all forms of nationalism (including Jewish nationalism), this did not in any way prevent him from proudly identifying himself as a Jew and as a man of science – who believed that the science that he founded, psychoanalysis, would triumph and withstand the most rigorous standards of rational criticism. I understand Freud to be affirming this basic conviction when he concludes his preface to the Hebrew translation of *Totem and Taboo* by declaring: "The author hopes, however, that he will be at one with his readers in the conviction that unprejudiced science cannot remain a stranger to the spirit of the new Jewry" (13:xv).

Despite the stylistic awkwardness, fragmentary quality, dubious historical claims, and gaps in Freud's "arguments," there is nevertheless a provocative grandeur about *The Man Moses and the Monotheistic Religion*. Much of what initially seems so confusing falls into place when we realize that the central issue that Freud is confronting is what he takes to be the quintessence of (his) Jewishness, its origins in Mosaic monotheism, and the psychological dynamics by which this religious tradition has been transmitted. Unfortunately most of the secondary literature dealing with Freud's *Moses* study has focused on what stands out as most scandalous – Freud's claim that Moses, the great "Jewish" leader was a foreigner, an Egyptian who created the Jews by compelling them to be followers of a purified Egyptian monotheism, and that it was the Jews who killed Moses in the wilderness. But I have argued that "this is not the whole story nor the most important part of the whole story" (23:17).

The most important part of the whole story is Freud's attempt to put into words what he felt with such strong emotional conviction. The Mosaic prohibition against images – the prophetic admonition not to fall back into idolatry, is not just a negative imperative. Positively, it is an expression of *Der Fortschritt in der Geistigkeit*. It is the ethical imperative to live a life of truth and justice. Freud did not waver in his conviction that the religious teachings of Judaism, like all religious teachings, were "neurotic relics," illusions which ought to be replaced with the "rational operation of the intellect." But he just as firmly argued that "[o]ur knowledge of the historical worth of certain religious doctrines increases our respect for them" (21:44). With the completion of *The Man Moses and the Monotheistic Religion*, Freud was fulfilling a personal quest that can be traced back to his earliest "engrossment in the Bible story," which began "almost as soon as I had learnt the art of reading" (20:8).[10] On the eve of "the final solution," a few months before his death, he was expressing what had eluded him for so long but which he emotionally felt so strongly – "his essential nature" as a Jew.

In order to tell "the whole story," Freud needed to answer the more general question of the psychological origins and dynamics of a religious tradition – an inquiry that he had begun in *Totem and Taboo*. Mosaic monotheism must itself be understood in the context of the development of religion from its origins in totemic religions through anthropomorphic polytheism, to the various forms of monotheism including its Egyptian sources, Judaism, and Christianity.

The reason why I have insisted upon the literal translation of the German title should now be fully clear. For the German title, *Der Mann Moses und die monotheistische Religion* underscores two key substantive points of the book. It was the *man*, the great man (*Der grosse Mann*) Moses who created the Jewish people.[11] Furthermore, the very redundancy of the phrase "*Die monotheistische Religion*" reminds us that monotheism must itself be understood in the context of the development of religions. We understand the "historical truth" of this purified monotheism when we trace its psychological origins back to the "historical truth" it distorts and displaces – the murder of the primal father in totemic religions. We can only fully appreciate the spiritual achievement of Mosaic monotheism when it is seen against the background of more "primitive" forms of religion.

It may seem paradoxical that Freud, who placed so much emphasis on images in the interpretation of dreams and phantasies, should be so critical of image making (and idolatry) when interpreting the psychological significance of the Mosaic prohibition against images. But when we understand his rationale for valorizing the triumph of abstract intellectuality over the "lower psychical activity" of sense perception, the paradox dissolves. Images *are* all important for psychoanalytic interpretation. They are essential data for any psychoanalytic interpretation. It is Freud who discovered just how much meaning is conveyed by fragmentary images which initially appear to be confused and meaningless. They are the clues for making inferences about unconscious mental processes. But what Freud emphasizes is the *psychoanalytic analysis* of these images, the complex patterns of reasoning and inferences that must be learned in order to interpret these images. Analysis may be interminable in the sense that it can never hope to achieve finality and certainty, it can never completely reveal the unconscious dynamics of the id. But this presents a challenge for further analysis – reaffirming Freud's (biblical) faith in the affirmation of speech and the potency of the word.

The whole story also demands a rethinking of the very concept of a religious tradition, especially as it pertains to the Jewish tradition. I deliberately use the expression "rethinking" because Freud himself is aware of the complex modalities by which a tradition is transmitted. His argument depends on the claim that the "half-forgotten tradition" of Mosaic monotheism, and its ethical message of living a life in truth and justice, was never completely obliterated. Like a *leitmotif*, Freud keeps returning to the significance of the biblical prophetic tradition in keeping alive the Mosaic ideal. But Freud's most distinctive (and controversial) contribution to understanding a religious tradition is to make us sensitive to the unconscious dimensions of this transmission. It is not what is "directly communicated" that is most important about a tradition. Or rather, even in direct communication, we must pay attention to what is unconsciously communicated. This is what leads Freud to refer to "unconscious memory-traces." I have argued that much of the discussion of Freud's "discredited Lamarckism" in *The Man Moses and the Monotheistic Religion* actually obscures the nuanced manner in which Freud is struggling to expand our understanding of how a religious tradition is transmitted. Specifically in regard to the Jewish tradition, Freud draws upon psychoanalytic concepts, especially the concepts of trauma, repression, latency, and the return of the repressed in order to account for the "historical truth" that is both concealed and revealed in the Jewish tradition.

At various stages in Freud's long career, he identifies with Athens and Rome. But in *The Man Moses and the Monotheistic Religion* – his last published book and testament – he identifies himself with Jerusalem. In retrospect, the words with which Freud concludes "*Der Fortschritt in der Geistigkeit*" have a special poignancy. Written at a time when the very survival of the Jewish people was more seriously threatened than at any other time in its history, Freud tells us:

The preference which through two thousand years the Jews have given to spiritual endeavour has, of course, had its effect; it has helped to build a dike against brutality and the inclination to violence which are usually found where athletic development becomes the ideal of the people. The harmonious development of spiritual and bodily activity, as achieved by the Greeks, was denied to the Jews. In this conflict their decision was at least made in favour of what is culturally the more important.[12]

CHAPTER 4

"Dialogue" with Yerushalmi[1]

Dear Yosef Hayim Yerushalmi,

For many years – long before the publication of your book, *Freud's Moses*, I have been deeply fascinated by *The Man Moses and the Monotheistic Religion*. As you well know, until the appearance of your own perceptive study, much of the discussion of Freud's last book has been highly polemical, and has not been very illuminating. Hostile critics, and even sympathetic readers, have tended to be dismissive. There has been a sharp critique of Freud's anthropological and ethnographic claims; and his historical reconstruction has been ridiculed as a "pure phantasy" with little (if any) objective evidence to support his claims. Subsequent research by historians, biblical scholars, Egyptologists, anthropologists, and ethnologists have seriously questioned many of his historical claims. Some commentators have tried to put Freud "on the couch," wildly speculating about his unconscious motives for writing such a scandalous book. Even those who have been most dedicated to Freud have written about the *Moses* book with a certain uneasy embarrassment – as if, at best, we should acknowledge that this is the work of an old man who was past his creative prime. I do not have to rehearse this depressing history of commentary and speculation because you have perceptively discussed it. Every reader of *The Man Moses and the Monotheistic Religion* (and every student of Freud) is indebted to you for raising the level of intellectual discussion – and for much more. You have brought your masterly knowledge of Jewish history and Jewish tradition to bear on the discussion. As an accomplished historian, you have uncovered all sorts of information that is relevant for interpreting and evaluating the *Moses* study. *Freud's Moses* is, in the best sense, thought-provoking. And yet, to be frank, I am not quite satisfied with your interpretation. I find that some of the points that you make in your four lectures and, especially, in your "Monologue with Freud," are not quite persuasive. At times, I do not think you do full justice to the meaning and power of Freud's claims. I even think there is a clear answer to the question that you raise in your final remarks – whether Anna Freud was speaking in her father's name when she stated in 1977 that "under present circumstances" characterizing psychoanalysis as a Jewish science "can serve as a title of honour." You ask "When your daughter conveyed those words to the congress in Jerusalem, *was she speaking in your name?*" (*FM*, 100). Only I suspect that Freud's answer might not quite be what you expect – and might even disappoint you. But this is to get ahead of myself. Let me indicate what I want to discuss with you. I want to focus on the questions and criticisms you raise about Freud's *Moses* book. There are other intriguing issues you explore: the relation between Freud and his father; the interpretation and significance of Jakob Freud's Hebrew inscription to the Philippsohn Bible, the gift which he "returned" to his son on the occasion of Sigmund's thirty-fifth birthday; and whether Freud concealed his knowledge of Hebrew and Yiddish. All of this is relevant for a judicious understanding of Freud's Jewish identity – but not always germane for evaluating the arguments presented in the *Moses* book. This is what I want to explore with you, primarily in regard to Freud's understanding of Jewish history and the Jewish tradition.

Like you, I think that we must pay close attention to Freud's "conscious intentions," and that we ought to examine what he actually says carefully. Otherwise, there is a danger of slipping into a patronizing attitude toward Freud – or worse. I would like to take a further turn in the rhetorical device that you employ so effectively, the Talmudic *le-didakh*. Quoting your own eloquent words, *le-didakh* "signifies that for the sake of the discussion and its effort to ascertain the truth, one party will provisionally accept the assumptions of the other, and they will go on from there" (*FM*, 83). Throughout this "dialogue," I will frequently quote from your text because I want to let you speak in your own words. One more preliminary before beginning. Jacques Derrida has already written perceptively about *Freud's Moses*, especially about your "Monologue with Freud."[2] I would like to draw him into our conversation at those points where his remarks supplement my own reservations about your text. So let me begin.

The first major point that you make in your "Monologue" concerns what you call "the pivot" of Freud's entire construction. Let me quote the words that you address to Freud:

You took it for granted, of course, that Moses' Egyptian origin and especially the trauma of his murder were repressed, forgotten, except as latent memories in the unconscious of the group, and it is here that you went astray. What eluded you was the most singular aspect of Jewish tradition from the Bible onward, to wit – its almost maddening refusal to conceal the misdeeds of the Jews . . . The vital question remains whether, if Moses had been murdered in the wilderness, *this* would have been forgotten or concealed. And here we must not merely speculate but contemplate directly, if briefly, some relevant aspects of Jewish tradition itself. (*FM*, 84)

According to you, "[n]o ancient scripture, epic, or chronicle . . . exposes the people that is its subject to the vilifications heaped repeatedly on Israel, the 'Chosen People,' in the Hebrew Bible" (*FM*, 84). You cite a number of instances to illustrate this, and refer to the famous passage in Numbers 14:10 where we are told that the Israelites stoned Moses and Aaron. Presumably, the Israelites would have stoned Moses and Aaron to death, if the Lord had not intervened. After referring to these passages and other passages from classical rabbinical literature which show that the rabbis "are fully persuaded that an attempt was made on the life of Moses" (*FM*, 85), you state your conclusion succinctly:

If Moses had actually been killed by our forefathers, not only would the murder not have been repressed but – on the contrary – it would have been remembered and recorded, eagerly and implacably, in the most vivid detail, the quintessential and ultimate exemplum of the sin of Israel's disobedience. (*FM*, 85)

The first point which I want to make is that you have not quite accurately represented what Freud says (as you acknowledge later). You write that Freud "took it for granted . . . that Moses' Egyptian origin and especially the trauma of his murder were repressed, forgotten, *except as latent memories in the unconscious of the group* . . ." (*FM*, 84, emphasis added). But in Freud's historical reconstruction, he tells us that the Levites who were the followers of Moses "remained loyal to their master, preserved his memory and carried out the tradition of his doctrines" (23:39). You quote this very sentence from Freud, but discount it when you write: "In fact, at one point in Part II of *Moses* you yourself wavered and assigned this role [those who knew about the murder and transmitted this knowledge] to the Levites" (*FM*, 88). I fail to see the basis for the judgment that Freud wavered. On the contrary, as you seem to suggest at other points in your "Monologue," Freud is expanding our sense of what constitutes a living tradition by emphasizing that there are both conscious and unconscious aspects of transmission of a tradition, although, of course, as a psychoanalyst, he is primarily concerned with the latter.

Furthermore, I find the claim that you make about what Freud took for "granted" perplexing, especially in light of your own discussion of the use that Freud made of the research of Ernst Sellin. Consider the way in which Freud characterizes Sellin's conclusions when he introduces the discussion of his work.

Then, in 1922, Ernst Sellin made a discovery which affected our problem decisively. He found in the Prophet Hosea (in the second half of the eighth century BC) unmistakable signs of a tradition to the effect that Moses, the founder of their religion, met with a violent end in a rising of his refractory and stiff-necked people, and that at the same time the religion he had introduced was thrown off. This tradition is not, however, restricted to Hosea; it reappears in most of the later Prophets, and indeed, according to Sellin, became the basis of all the later Messianic expectations. (23:36)

The issue that I want to focus on here is not the credibility of Sellin's claims, nor Freud's interpretation of them, but whether you have accurately represented Freud's views. To quote you, "the issue for the moment is not what we think, but what he thought" (*HN*, 386). The reason why I think you are inaccurate (or at least not precise) is because Freud certainly does not take it for granted that the Egyptian origin of Moses and the trauma of his murder were "repressed, forgotten, except as latent memories in the unconscious of the group" (*FM*, 84). There is no doubt in the above passages that Freud thought that the Levite followers of the Egyptian Moses kept alive the memory of his origin and his murder. Furthermore, based on Sellin's historical interpretation of the Prophets – something that Freud does *not* take for granted – Freud suggests that there was an explicit (conscious) tradition in which the murder of Moses was known – at least by the priests. In short, Freud thought that there was an élite who were fully aware of the fact that Moses had been murdered by the Hebrews. I hope you will not consider this a mere quibble, especially in light of your own scrupulous demands to be faithful to Freud's text, to what he actually says. I will show that this is not a minor point but has significant consequences for the way in which you represent – and slightly distort – what Freud means by tradition, the unconscious, repression, the return of the repressed, and memory-traces. But let me proceed methodically.

You might respond that Freud's claim that there were those who knew about the murder of Moses (and transmitted this knowledge) does not alter the substance of your argument. If Freud had a better understanding of "the essential character of Jewish tradition" (*FM*, 86), he would have realized that the murder of Moses would not have been concealed. It is unimaginable to think that such a momentous event would have been deliberately concealed, especially in light of "the most singular aspect of Jewish tradition from the Bible onward, to wit – its almost maddening refusal to conceal the misdeeds of the Jews" (*FM*, 84). This brings us – employing your own phrase – to the question of "the essential character of Jewish tradition." And here of course, your sophisticated knowledge of the Jewish tradition is far superior to Freud's rather superficial understanding. But there is a prior question lurking in the background – what philosophers sometimes call a "conceptual" question. How is one to understand a religious tradition?

At one point in your lectures you say that what readers of Freud's book have "failed to recognize" is that "the true axis of the book . . . is the problem of tradition, not merely its origins, but above all its dynamics" (*FM*, 29). I completely agree with you. But before taking up the issue of the *Jewish* tradition, I want to explore with you the more general question of Freud's understanding of a *religious* tradition. Once again I want to bracket the question of the *validity* of Freud's claims. If criticism is to be on target then the first task is to represent accurately what Freud says.

I think you would agree that (a) Freud believed that in order to gain a deeper understanding of Judaism as a monotheistic religion, we must examine it in the more general context of the *development* of religions; (b) monotheism was predated by a variety of polytheistic religions; (c) the "origin" of religious phenomena can be traced back to "totemic religion," which itself arose as a consequence of the murder of the father by the band of brothers in the primal horde. Whatever "we" may think about this narrative, Freud thought he had discovered a continuous motif in this development – where the central event in paternalistic religions (leaving aside maternal religious phenomena) is the repetition of the murder of the father figure. This is true for the "father-religion" of Judaism and the Christian "son-religion." "Christianity, having arisen out of a father-religion, became a son-religion. It has not escaped the fate of having to get rid of the father"(23:136).

Freud's approach to religious phenomena is based upon the centrality of the Oedipus complex in psychoanalytic theory. In every generation, there is a deep psychological ambivalence of sons toward their fathers and their father figures. Every son has to deal with this psychological ambivalence – and this means that he has to deal with his (unconscious) murderous feelings toward his father. You may want to challenge and criticize this psychoanalytic understanding of paternalistic religious traditions – and it has been seriously questioned. But in the section (*FM*, 83-4) when you accuse Freud of "ignoring the essential character of the Jewish tradition," you have not advanced any arguments to show that Freud is mistaken in his understanding of what he takes to be characteristic of (paternalistic) religions. You may think that I am not being quite fair to what you intended in your discussion of the "essential character of the Jewish tradition" – that it was not your intention (in this context) to raise general questions about Freud's understanding of religious phenomena and the development of religious traditions, but rather to underscore what has been a dominant characteristic of the *Jewish* tradition.

But let me indicate what makes me so uneasy and skeptical about your reasoning here. Your trump card is the appeal to "the essential character of the Jewish tradition." But I fail to see that this by itself is decisive because, what is at stake here, are *competing* conceptions of this "essential character." For Freud, the "essential character" of the Jewish *religious* tradition – like all paternalistic religions – involves the trauma of the murder of the father figure. He may be mistaken, and you may be right about the Jewish tradition. But the issue is not going to be resolved by assertions and counter-assertions, without a detailed argument about what constitutes a religious tradition, and whether the Jewish religious tradition is or is not an exception to Freud's analysis of father religions. Even if one agrees with you that in the Jewish tradition there is no *deliberate* (i.e. conscious) attempt to conceal the misdeeds of the Jewish people, this is not directly relevant to challenging Freud's claims about the unconscious dynamics of repression. *Repression is not conscious suppression.* It is a cardinal principle of psychoanalysis that the logic of consciousness is fundamentally different from the logic of the unconscious. In short, the burden of proof is on you to show that Freud is wrong in his analysis of the unconscious dynamics of repression – that the repression of murderous intentions is not applicable to Judaism.

At this point I would like to bring Derrida into our conversation. He also cites the passage from your "Monologue" that I quoted above – the passage in which you categorically assert that if Moses had been killed by the forefathers of the Jews, this misdeed would have been recorded in the most vivid detail. He then raises a series of questions and issues – which I would also like to raise.

How can Yerushalmi be sure that the murder in question has not been abundantly recalled and archived ("remembered and recorded") in the

memory of Israel? How can he claim to *prove* an absence of archive? How does
one prove in general an absence of archive, if not in relying on classical norms
(presence/absence of literal and explicit reference to this or to that, to a this or
to a that which one supposes to be identical to themselves, and simply absent,
actually absent, if they are not simply present, *actually* present; how can one not,
and why not, take into account *unconscious*, and more generally *virtual* archives)?
Now Yerushalmi knows very well that Freud's intention is to analyze, across the
apparent absence of memory and of archive, all kinds of symptoms, signs,
figures, metaphors, and metonymies that attest, at least virtually, an archival
documentation where the "ordinary historian" identifies none. *Whether one goes
along with him or not in his demonstration, Freud claimed that the murder of Moses effectively
left archives, documents, symptoms in the Jewish memory and even in the memory of humanity.
Only the texts of this archive are not readable according to the paths of "ordinary history" and
this is the very relevance of psychoanalysis, if it has one.* (*AF*, 64–5, emphasis in last seven
lines added)

The "pivot" (to use your own expression) of Freud's "entire construction" is that there are all sorts of traces and signs of this scandalous
event. This is the point of the famous passage in which he compares a
text to a murder and tells us how difficult it is to eliminate all its traces.
It is because this murder was "recorded" – although not in the manifest
ways that would immediately be recognized by "ordinary historians" –
that Freud is able to play the role of a psychoanalytic detective. Of
course, it may be objected that it is Freud who has misread the signs,
and that he has not made an "historical" discovery, but rather projec-
ted his phantasy onto historical events. But this needs to be shown and
argued.

Ironically, Freud might completely agree with you. You are right! It is
"the essential character of Jewish tradition" to record the misdeeds of
the Jews in "vivid detail." The issue would then turn on what constitutes
recording an event in vivid detail. You seem to assume – without
justifying the assumption – that recording an event in vivid detail is the
same as making it manifestly obvious. But is not Freud arguing that
repressed events of traumatic experiences are recorded in "vivid detail,"
yet that it requires psychoanalytic sophistication to interpret this "vivid
detail"? This is the main thrust of Derrida's claim when he says that
(according to Freud) there are texts of this archive which psychoanalysis
teaches us to read. Indeed, one might state Freud's case in even stronger
terms. It is only because the murder of Moses was recorded in the most
vivid detail that he is able to reconstruct what happened. Let us recall
what Freud says about the double meaning of *Entstellung* (distortion). For
Entstellung means "to change the appearance of something" and "to put

something in another place, to displace." "Accordingly, in many instances of textual distortion, we may nevertheless count upon finding
what has been suppressed and disavowed hidden away somewhere else,
though changed and torn from its context. Only it will not always be
easy to recognize it" (23:43).

In this same section, you write "As for Moses being an Egyptian,
what's in a name? Both Philo and Josephus knew that the name Moses is
etymologically Egyptian, but they did not conclude from this that he was
of Egyptian stock" (*FM*, 85). I have no wish to defend the flimsy
etymological argument with which Freud begins his book. In fairness to
Freud, it should be noted, that after presenting this argument, he does
say: "Our investigations might have had to rest content with this
inconclusive and, moreover, uncertain outcome, and they might have
done nothing towards answering the question of whether Moses was an
Egyptian" (23:14). But I would like to use the opportunity to explore a
possibility which you do not consider. We are both familiar with the
letter that Freud wrote to Arnold Zweig in 1934 in which he stated: "The
fact that I wrote at length to you in an earlier letter about Moses being
an Egyptian is not the essential point, though it is a starting point"
(*SFAZ*, 98). There is, of course, little doubt that Freud did think that
Moses was an Egyptian. But I would like to suggest the following
thought experiment. Imagine that Freud admitted that he was mistaken
about this, and that he conceded that Moses was actually a Hebrew.
Would such an admission significantly alter Freud's *psychoanalytic* account of what presumably happened in the wilderness? My hunch is
that this would make very little substantive difference. Let me explain.
According to Freud, the Jews killed Moses *not* because he was an
Egyptian, but because he compelled them to follow a rigorous monotheistic religion against which they were rebelling. It is the trauma of this
murder that has psychoanalytic significance for Freud. Of course, Freud
would have had to come up with some other explanation of how Moses
arrived at his monotheistic convictions. But Freud does not claim to give
an adequate explanation of the "origin" of monotheism, for – as he
himself noted – he has not even provided an adequate account of how
Akhenaten arrived at his monotheistic beliefs. Freud would also have to
modify some of the things he says about the introduction of the custom
of circumcision – but not by much. For he could just as well have
claimed that even a (Hebrew) Moses who led the Jews out of Egypt
appropriated the Egyptian practice of circumcision in order to enhance
the self-esteem of the slaves that he was leading out of bondage.

I am *not* suggesting that Freud actually entertained this alternative hypothesis. My main point is that the distinctively psychoanalytic interpretation that Freud offers for the rationale and consequences of the murder of Moses is conceptually independent of the question of whether Moses was or was not an Egyptian. In this more radical sense, we can say with Freud that the hypothesis that Moses was an Egyptian is only a "starting point."

Returning to the remark that Freud made in his letter to Arnold Zweig, we may ask if "Moses being an Egyptian is not the essential point," what then is the essential point? A quick response would be that it is the (alleged) fact that the Jews murdered Moses. But strictly speaking, this is also *not* accurate. It is not the murder of Moses that is the essential point, but Freud's claim that this was a *traumatic* experience for the Jews. It is the distinctively Freudian understanding of trauma, and his claim that it was the traumatic reaction to the murder of Moses, that is the "essential point." This understanding of the centrality of trauma is the very basis for the analogy that Freud draws between the history of the Jewish religion and "the genesis of human neuroses." Once we understand what Freud means by trauma, then this opens up still other possibilities which neither you nor Freud explore.

When Freud introduces his discussion of trauma in Part III of the *Moses* book, he tells us, "We give the name of *traumas* to those *impressions*, experienced early and later forgotten, to which we attach such great importance in the aetiology of the neuroses" (23:72, emphasis added).[3] It is not the dateable event itself, but the psychological reaction to an alleged event that is crucial for Freud's distinctive understanding of trauma. "We must often resign ourselves to saying that all we have before us is an unusual, abnormal reaction to experiences and demands which affect everyone, but are worked over and dealt with by other people in another manner which may be called normal" (23:72–3). Consider the consequences of this understanding of trauma. Freud recognizes that there are events which may be traumatic for one person but which are not traumatic for another. What is even more important is that insofar as Freud places the emphasis on *impressions* rather than on the events themselves as the primary *causal* factor in the genesis of a trauma, the question of whether a given historical event did or did not occur begins to recede in its importance. Suppose, in the spirit of Freud, we continue to apply this analogy to Freud's account of Jewish history, and specifically to the question of whether Moses was in fact murdered by the Jews. Pursuing this line of reasoning, it is not even necessary to say that it was the actual murder of Moses that was the cause of the trauma experienced by the Jewish people. The fact that there was a deep unconscious hostility toward Moses; that the Israelites were ambivalent toward their great awe-inspiring leader; that they felt a murderous hatred which they could not *consciously* acknowledge would be sufficient to trigger the trauma.

There is an unsuspected irony that results from this line of reasoning. You point out that there is clear evidence in the biblical narrative that the Hebrews had murderous feelings toward Moses, and that a serious attempt was made to murder Moses. You also write: "Indeed the rabbis in the Midrash are fully persuaded that an attempt was made on the life of Moses, and they make this more explicit than does the biblical text" (*FM*, 85).

I want to make it perfectly clear that I am not claiming that Freud himself says what I have been emphasizing. We know that if he had never published Part III, if all we had to go on were the first two essays that were published in *Imago*, then one would think – as many commentators have – that Freud's essential claims are that Moses was an Egyptian and that he was murdered by the Jews. Strictly speaking, neither of these are really essential. There is an ambiguity in Freud about whether it is a (datable) event that is the cause of a trauma or whether it is primarily the reaction – the psychological *impression* of an alleged event that is the primary causal factor. (There are even some parallels with the debate concerning the significance of Freud's abandonment of the "seduction theory.") It is clear, however, that unless there is a distinctive psychological impression, there is no trauma. Furthermore, there is plenty of biblical evidence of murderous feelings on the part of the Israelites – the "murmurings" of the Israelites in the wilderness – and indeed, the report of an actual attempt to murder Moses. These feelings and this intent to murder Moses (which even you emphasize) are sufficient to trigger a traumatic reaction, especially given the psychological ambivalence toward Moses. Once again I would like to draw Derrida into our discussion. For he makes a similar point from a slightly different angle.

Yerushalmi seems to conclude – and to want to convince Professor Freud – that if in fact they [the Israelites] wanted to kill Moses (and Aaron), and if this intention has indeed remained in the memory and in the archive, what counts is that the Israelites did not "actually" kill him. This conclusion appears to be doubly fragile. And even from the Midrash point of view in question. First, without needing to convoke psychoanalysis yet, one should recognize that if the murder did not take place, if it remained virtual, if it only almost took place, *the intention to kill was effective, actual, and in truth accomplished*. There was acting out, the stones were thrown *in fact*, they continued to be thrown while only divine intervention intercepted them. The crime was not interrupted at any moment by Israelites themselves, going no further than their suspended intention, or renouncing in the face of the sin. There was thus not only *intention* but *attempt* to murder, *effective, actual* attempt, which only an exterior cause (a jurist would say an accident) diverted. Second, and this time taking into account a psychoanalytic logic, what difference is there between a murder and an intention to murder (above all if it is acted out, but even if it is not murder, even if the intention does not become attempt to murder)? Murder begins with the intention to kill. The unconscious does not know the difference here between the virtual and the actual, the intention and the action (a certain Judaism also, by the way), or at least does not model itself on the manner in which the conscious (as well as the law or the morals accorded to it) distributes the relations of the virtual, of the intentional, and of the actual . . . In any case, the unconscious may have kept the memory and the archive of the intention to kill, of the acting out of this desire to kill (as it is attested by the texts Yerushalmi himself cites, in particular this singular *Midrash*) – even if there has been repression; because a repression also archives that of which it dissimulates or encrypts the archives. What is more, we see well that the repression was not all that efficient: the will to kill, the acting out and the attempt to murder are avowed, they are literally inscribed in the archive. If Moses was not killed, it is only thanks to God. Left to themselves, the Israelites, who wanted to kill Moses, would have killed him: they did everything to kill him. (*AF*, 65–6)

You may wish to protest. You seem to think that Freud's views are based on a "discredited Lamarckism." But before taking up this objection, I want to consider the issues raised by Derrida from a slightly different perspective.

There are (at least) three alleged murders that play a fundamental role in Freud's narrative of the development of religion: the murder of the primal father; the murder of Moses; and the murder of Jesus. Although Freud claims that the latter two are unconscious repetitions of the "original" murder, the reaction to each of these murders has very different consequences for religion. Each is a crucial event in the formation of different stages of religion: the first for totemic religions; the second for Judaism; and the third for Christianity. Freud's claims are even more ambitious, for he argues that the murder of the primal father is the formative event not only for religion, but for the origin of society and ethics. It is at once disturbing and humbling to realize that this act of violence is a condition for the very genesis of religion and ethics. Disturbing, because without this first crime there would be no social organization, no recognition of mutual obligations – no morality and justice (13:82). And it is humbling, because Freud is claiming that we should not forget that the "beginning of morality and justice" is intimately related to violence – indeed murder. (In this respect, there are affinities with Nietzsche, Benjamin, Derrida, and Arendt.) The question arises whether we are to take Freud's claims about these murders as the literal or "material truth." Does the murder of the primal father have the same factual status as the murders of John F. Kennedy or Martin Luther King Jr., where there is plenty of objective evidence that these events took place – at specific times and places? Here is where the problems begin.

In his *Moses* book (23:53) and in his correspondence, Freud states that *The Man Moses and the Monotheistic Religion* is a continuation of the theme of *Totem and Taboo* in application to Jewish religious history. By considering what Freud says about the murder of the primal father, we may gain some insight into the alleged murder of Moses. Freud, of course, is aware that he is postulating such a murder; it is an inference. He does not assert that there is direct objective historical evidence to support such a claim. He tells us: "The determination of the original state of things thus invariably remains a matter of construction" (13:103). Freud's construction is not based solely on what he appropriates from Darwin, Atkinson, and Robertson Smith (23:81–4); it is also based on his observation that "we attribute the same emotional attitudes to these primitive men that we are able to establish by analytic investigation in the primitives of the present day – in our children" (23:81–2). Even more importantly, it is based upon the clinical observation of neurotics. It is this analogy with neurotics that presents a problem for Freud – one which he addresses in the last few paragraphs of *Totem and Taboo*. Freud says that we find in neurotic patients guilt and atonement for crimes that they have not committed. When we probe a bit, we find there were no such crimes in fact, but only impulses and emotions.

What lie behind the sense of guilt of neurotics are always *psychical* realities and never *factual* ones. What characterizes neurotics is that they prefer psychical to factual reality and react just as seriously to thoughts as normal people do to realities.

May not the same have been true of primitive men? . . . Accordingly the mere hostile *impulse* against the father, the mere existence of a wishful *phantasy* of killing and devouring him, would have been enough to produce the moral reaction that created totemism and taboo. In this way we should avoid the necessity for deriving the origin of our cultural legacy, of which we justly feel so proud, from a hideous crime, revolting to all our feelings. No damage would thus be done to the causal chain stretching from the beginning to the present day, for psychical reality would be strong enough to bear the weight of these consequences. (13:159–60)

The parallel with the murder of Moses is clear. From a psychoanalytic perspective, it is the *psychical* reality that is decisive. This psychical reality does not presuppose the "actual" murder of Moses, although it certainly does presuppose the *factual* reality of murderous feelings, emotions, and intentions. (As you point out, there is plenty of evidence in the Hebrew Bible and the Rabbinic tradition that there were such impulses, emotions, and intentions.)

Freud does not simply leave us with the suggestion that there may never have been an actual murder of the primal father. Let us closely follow his reasoning. The question that seems so fundamental for us (and, for you) is the apparently categorical difference between intention and execution. You do not dispute the intention, but the deed – insisting that if the murder of Moses had actually taken place it would have been recorded. As you tell us: "the most singular aspect of Jewish tradition from the Bible onward [is] its almost maddening refusal to conceal the misdeeds of the Jews" (*FM*, 84).

But Freud takes a different tack. He says:

Here we are faced by a *decision* which is indeed no easy one. First, however, it must be confessed that the distinction [between intentions and their execution], which may seem fundamental to other people, *does not in our judgment affect the heart of the matter*. If wishes and impulses have been the full value of facts for primitive men, it is our business to give their attitude our understanding attention instead of correcting it in accordance with our own standards. (13:160, emphasis added)

So Freud suggests that we take a closer look at the analogy that has led him to the "present uncertainty" about whether there really was such "a hideous crime." What Freud now says is even more illuminating. He declares:

It is not accurate to say that obsessional neurotics, weighed down under the burden of an excessive morality, are defending themselves only against *psychical* reality and are punishing themselves for impulses which were merely *felt*. *Historical* reality has a share in the matter as well. In their childhood they had these evil impulses pure and simple, and turned them into acts so far as the impotence of childhood allowed. (13:161)

In this context the "historical reality" refers to the childhood experiences of obsessional neurotics. Children do not (ordinarily) succeed in murdering their fathers – although in their childlike manner they may attempt to act out their "evil impulses." Drawing the parallel to the Semites in the wilderness, it is "factually" important that a serious attempt was made to murder their leader, Moses – not that they were successful in executing this deed. And again, you do not deny this. You (and the rabbis) affirm this.

Freud is making several key points in these concluding passages from *Totem and Taboo*. First, the most important causal factor in the story of the murder of the primal father is the *psychical* reality; a psychical reality that is not based on mere phantasies but on the actual attempt to murder the primal father. Second, it is not easy to decide whether there really was a murder or only the intention and the attempt to murder. Third, from a psychoanalytic perspective, the distinctions we normally make between intention, attempt, and deed do not have the significance that they have in other contexts – for example, juridical contexts.

Freud concludes his discussion by pointing out that if he has to make a decision, if he has to come down on one side or the other, he would decide that the murder of the primal father actually happened. The reason that he gives for this decision is based on the *differences* between obsessive neurotics and primitive men.

Nor must we let ourselves be influenced too far in our judgment of primitive men by the analogy of neurotics. There are distinctions, too, which must be borne in mind. It is no doubt true that the sharp contrast that we make between thinking and doing is absent in both of them. But neurotics are above all *inhibited* in their actions: with them the thought is a complete substitute for the deed. Primitive men, on the other hand, are *uninhibited*: Thought passes directly into action. With them it is rather the deed that is the substitute for the thought. And that is why, without laying claim to any finality of judgment, I think that in the case before us it may safely be assumed that 'in the beginning was the Deed'. (13:161)

It may be objected that Freud here is addressing himself to the specific question of the murder of the primal father, and he is not speaking about the murder of Moses by the Semites. But I do not think this objection really has much force because the "psychoanalytic logic" of the two situations is the same. As Derrida says (just as the Hebrew Bible tells us) "[t]here was thus not only *intention* but *attempt* to murder, *effective, actual* attempt, which only an exterior cause . . . diverted." Nothing crucial in Freud's psychoanalytic account of the murderous intentions of the Semites toward their leader, the repression of these "evil impulses," and the ultimate consequences of this repression in shaping the character of the Jewish people, depends on establishing that at a specific historical time in a specific physical place, the man Moses (if he ever actually existed) was actually murdered.

Freud does maintain, however, that regardless of the decision we make about the factual status of the murder of the primal father, there is nevertheless the memory of such a murder. And furthermore, this murder was "acted out" again in the alleged murder of Moses. So even if we assume that the actual deed – the physical murder of Moses – never took place, there have still been unconscious memory-traces of this "deed" transmitted through generations of the Jewish people. It is this claim that you also criticize when you accuse Freud of basing his understanding of the transmission of a religious tradition on dubious Lamarckian assumptions of the transmission of acquired characteristics.

Addressing yourself to Professor Freud, you say:

Tantalizing though it may be, your notion of a tradition transmitted through the unconscious of the group, even if only during a period of "latency," is impossible to accept, and not only because of modern genetics or molecular biology. There are differences between individual and collective memory so fundamental as to be unbridgeable by the analogy you have proposed . . .

Though it is composed of individuals, the group does not possess the organic unity and continuity of the least of its members, who can remember, forget, and recall his or her personal experiences . . .

Peoples, groups, at any given time or in any generation, can only "remember" a past that has been actively transmitted to them, and which they have accepted as meaningful. Conversely, a people "forgets" when the generation that currently possesses the past does not convey it to the next or when the latter rejects what it has received and does not pass it onward. (*FM*, 87–8)

I believe that these paragraphs express the core of your objections to Freud's understanding of a religious tradition. I also think – with all due respect – that you are doing Freud an injustice. For these passages reflect a basic misunderstanding of what Freud is saying and showing in the *Moses* book. I want to analyze your statements carefully, in order to illuminate what is so powerful and challenging in Freud's discussion.

Let me begin with a point that you reiterate over and over again – your criticism of Freud's Lamarckism. The first time (at least to my knowledge) that you stated this critical point was in your 1986 postscript to *Zakhor*. In that context, you write:

As the "life of a people" is a biological metaphor, so the "memory of a people" is a psychological metaphor – unless one personifies the group as an organism endowed with a collective psyche whose functions correspond in every way to that of the individual – which is to say, unless one chooses to read history with Freud and face the consequences of a now discredited psycho-Lamarckism.[4]

In your footnote to this passage, you direct the reader to *Totem and Taboo*, *Civilization and its Discontents*, and above all *Moses and Monotheism*(Z, 145), without giving any specific indication of which passages in these works are evidence for the "now discredited psycho-Lamarckism." In the second sentence of your article "Freud on the 'Historical Novel': From the Manuscript Draft (1934) of Moses and Monotheism" you declare: "Rejected by historians and anthropologists alike, its psycho-Lamarckian assumptions in utter disrepute, for some time now it has seemed that the only way to salvage the book is to treat it primarily as a psychological document of Freud's inner life" (*HN*, 375).

And in *Freud's Moses*, you write: "Nowhere is Freud's Lamarckism more striking and radical than in *Moses and Monotheism*" (*FM*, 30). In order to underscore the absurdity of Freud's position, you write (in a passage that I quoted earlier): "The archaic heritage of human beings, Freud insists in *Moses and Monotheism*, 'comprises not only dispositions but subject matter – memory-traces of the experience of earlier generations.' At which point even the most ardent and loyal admirer of Freud can only whisper to himself, 'Certum, quia absurdum est'" (*FM*, 31).

The first observation that I want to make is that you keep repeating this criticism without ever pausing to explain what *you* mean by "Lamarckism" or "psycho-Lamarckism." You write as if it were perfectly clear what is meant by these highly contested expressions – as if it were an undisputed fact that Freud makes "psycho-Lamarckian" assumptions which are in "utter disrepute." When you do make occasional remarks about the transmission of "acquired characters" or the "genetics of modern biology," these tend to be casual and offhand. Given the care and sensitivity with which you treat Freud's texts, I find it surprising that you keep reiterating the accusation of Lamarckism without analyzing its meaning(s) or offering specific textual evidence to support your claims. I have already discussed why I (and Derrida) think it is misleading to claim that in *The Man Moses and the Monotheistic Religion* Freud's Lamarckism is "striking and radical." I do not want to repeat myself. (See pp. 46–58). But I would like to make a few general points. The entire question of Freud's attraction to and understanding of Lamarckism is extremely complex – much more complex than you indicate. A full-scale analysis of the issues involved would require a detailed discussion of the texts you cite as evidence (including *A*

Phylogenetic Fantasy: Overview of the Transference Neurosis), as well as a careful review of the exchanges between Freud and Ferenczi when they entertained the possibility of writing jointly about Lamarckism. Freud's understanding of Lamarckism is unconventional and even idiosyncratic. Furthermore, I have suggested that you have a tendency to conflate what ought to be carefully distinguished: strong and weak Lamarckism. It is *you*, not Freud, who speak about the "encoding within the genetic legacy of a particular group" (*FM*, 31). This is what I mean by "strong Lamarckism." And the reason why the expression "weak Lamarckism" might even be considered to be a misnomer is because the transmission of a culture or a tradition means that there is the transmission of "acquired characters."

Frankly, I do not see why the claim that the archaic heritage of human beings "comprises not only dispositions but subject matter – memory-traces of the experiences of earlier generations" is *by itself* absurd or Lamarckian. I do not want to deny that, in some sense, Freud, to the end of his life, held views that bear a strong affinity with Lamarck's emphasis on the phylogenetic transmission of "acquired characters." But our attention should be directed to the question of what *precisely* is the substantive content of Freud's alleged "psycho-Lamarckism," and whether Freud's understanding of the transmission of an archaic heritage is dependent on a "discredited" Lamarckism. In other words, even if Freud held Lamarckian and psycho-Lamarckian beliefs, one must scrutinize the role that these beliefs play in his understanding about the transmission of memory-traces.

But rather than get distracted by the tangled and complex questions concerning whether (and in what sense) Freud was or was not a Lamarckian, let me speak directly to what I find most troubling about your unqualified remarks.

Wittgenstein, in his *Philosophical Investigations*, makes an extremely perceptive remark about "pictures" that hold us captive. He does not ridicule this tendency. He knows how deep and gripping such "pictures" can be. Philosophy as an activity is likened to a form of therapy directed toward loosening the hold that these compulsive pictures have upon us. Now, I believe that you are the captive of a "picture" of Freudian theory which is a distorted one – especially concerning Freud's understanding of the unconscious. So I want to begin by reconstructing this picture (sticking close to your own words).

You write that Freud "personifies the group as an organism endowed with a collective psyche whose functions correspond in every way to that of the individual" (*Z*, 109). Furthermore, when Freud draws his analogy between the role of trauma in the aetiology of an individual's neurosis and the trauma of the murder of Moses in the history of the Jewish people, you say that "[c]ollectively the group too represses the memory of profound events experienced early in its history and transmits them phylogenetically through the unconscious, 'independent of direct communication,' until what was repressed occasionally breaks forth much later in distorted form but with utterly compelling force" (*FM*, 30). According to you Freud is committed to the thesis that there was a genetic encoding of the trauma of Moses' murder which was subsequently biologically transmitted to future generations (this is the heart of his supposed "discredited Lamarckism"). Elaborating on this "picture," you seem to think that Freud is committed to the idea of the "transmission of a tradition . . . as a totally unconscious process." And you flatly deny that it is possible to explain the transmission of a tradition in this way.

Though much of the process of transmission may be nonverbal, that is not tantamount of its being unconscious. The basic modalities in the continuity of a religious tradition are precept and example, narrative, gesture, ritual, and certainly all of these act upon, and are interpreted by, not only consciousness but the unconscious. The true challenge for psychoanalysis is not to plunge the entire history of tradition into a hypothetical group unconscious, but to help clarify, in a nonreductive way, what unconscious needs are being satisfied at any given time by living within a given religious tradition, by believing its myths and performing its rites. (*FM*, 89)

The fact that Freud takes his "stand upon the reality of an archaic unconscious inheritance forged out of the historical experience of our ancestors and transmitted 'independently of direct communication and education by example'" has "superlative interest" for you (*FM*, 89). So much so that this is one of the few places in your book where you feel compelled to shift the discussion from Freud's texts to his psychological needs. You write: "[b]ut I am almost . . . persuaded that it [the stand that Freud takes] . . . served a powerful inner personal need" (*FM*, 89).

Before examining the above statements, I want to consider some marginal but relevant issues. Given Freud's deep skepticism about anything resembling a Jungian "collective unconscious," as well as his explicit statement: "I do not think we gain anything by introducing the concept of a 'collective unconscious'" (23:132), I am surprised that you say – without any qualification – that Freud "personifies the group as an organism endowed with a collective psyche whose functions correspond in every way to that of the individual." Furthermore, you seem to disregard Freud's explicit warning: "We cannot at first sight say in what form this past existed during the time of its eclipse. It is not easy for us to carry over the concepts of individual psychology into group psychology . . ." (23:132). Taking this warning seriously might have qualified your categorical claim that Freud postulates "a collective psyche whose functions corresponded *in every way* to that of an individual."

I am also perplexed that you do not give sufficient prominence to the many passages in which Freud says that the religion of Moses did not disappear without leaving a trace. Freud is certainly not speaking about any pseudo-scientific genetic encoding of memory-traces when he writes:

The religion of Moses, however, had not disappeared without leaving a trace. A kind of memory of it had survived, obscured and distorted, supported, perhaps, among individual members of the priestly caste by ancient records. And it was this tradition of a great past which continued to work in the background, as it were, which gradually gained more and more power over men's minds, and which finally succeeded in transforming the god Yahweh into the god of Moses and in calling back to life the religion of Moses which had been established and then abandoned long centuries earlier. (23:124)

I have asked myself why it is that you ignore or play down those passages which conflict with your Lamarckian reading, as well as those passages in which Freud explicitly indicates that there are disanalogies between the aetiology of neurosis in the individual and the religious life of a people. I would like to suggest a hypothesis. I think that the heart of the matter is the way you understand what Freud means by the unconscious and unconscious processes. At one point you speak of a "totally unconscious process." The very phrasing here suggests that you are thinking of the unconscious as a region that is "totally" cut off from consciousness. This is what makes you so uneasy about Freud's appeal to "unconscious memory-traces." For if "memory-traces" were "totally unconscious" in the sense that they were forever beyond our conscious lives and left no trace on our conscious lives, then this would be absurd. What I find missing from your discussion is a nuanced understanding of the unconscious whereby the unconscious is *never* totally cut off from our conscious lives; it always leaves its traces. And yet, at other times, you are extremely perceptive about Freud's nuanced understanding of unconscious mental processes.[5] It is sometimes said that Freud's great discovery was the unconscious. I have always felt that this is extremely misleading. Many other thinkers before Freud postulated unconscious mental processes. It is not the unconscious, but its dynamics (and especially the devious and complex ways in which unconscious processes subtly influence our conscious lives) that is Freud's great contribution. The introduction of the topographical model of id, ego, and super-ego furthers our understanding of the complex interplay of unconscious and conscious processes. Of course, the unconscious is not to be confused with the preconscious, and it certainly is not the case that we can make all unconscious processes available to our consciousness – even in the most successful analysis. (This is one reason why analysis is terminable and interminable.) But the very phrase "totally unconscious" can be misleading insofar as it suggests some rigid ontological separation between what is conscious and unconscious. You may even agree with my description of the subtle Freudian interplay between conscious and unconscious processes, and wonder why I think it is relevant to your critical reservations about Freud. So let me explain.

You not only strongly object to Freud's assertion that "the archaic heritage of human beings comprises not only dispositions but also subject-matter – memory-traces of the experience of earlier generations," but you also object to Freud's claim that:

I have behaved for a long time as though the inheritance of memory-traces of the experience of our ancestors, independently of direct communication and of the influence of education by the setting of an example, were established beyond question. When I spoke of the survival of a tradition among a people or of the formation of a people's character, I had mostly in mind an inherited tradition of this kind and not transmitted by communication. (23:99–100)

You interpret this passage as evidence of Freud's "discredited Lamarckism," and as a misguided understanding of a religious tradition and how it is transmitted. Let me cite once again the passage in which you indicate how you understand a religious tradition, and what the potential value of psychoanalysis might be for understanding a religious tradition.

It seems to me, however, that the potential value of psychoanalysis to the understanding of religious tradition does not reside in such precarious postulates. One cannot explain the transmission of a tradition at any time as a totally unconscious process. Though much of the process of transmission may be nonverbal, that is not tantamount to its being unconscious. The basic modalities in the continuity of a religious tradition are precept and example, narrative, gesture, ritual, and certainly all of these act upon, and are interpreted by, not only consciousness but the unconscious. The true challenge for psychoanalysis is not to plunge the entire history of tradition into a hypothetical group unconscious, but to help to clarify, in a nonreductive way, what unconscious needs are being satisfied at any given time by living within a given religious tradition, by believing its myths and performing its rites. And that task, which would also help us to understand the changes in the evolution of tradition, has hardly begun. (*FM*, 89)

This is a strange passage – one in which it is not Freud but Yerushalmi who is wavering. Even though rhetorically, it is presented as if it were an objection to Freud, it actually echoes much of what Freud affirms. Freud does *not* say that the transmission of a tradition is "a totally unconscious process." He argues for an expanded sense of tradition that does justice to both conscious and unconscious aspects of its transmission. The great interpreter of dreams is not someone who needs to be instructed that the "nonverbal" is not to be identified with the "unconscious." There certainly is no dispute between you and Freud that the modalities for the transmission of tradition "are interpreted by not only consciousness but by the unconscious." (Once again you take a swipe at Freud for presumably postulating a "group unconscious" even though he explicitly disclaims this.) When you go on to say that "[t]he true challenge for psychoanalysis is . . . to help clarify . . . what unconscious needs are being satisfied at any given time by living within a given religious tradition, by believing its myths and performing its rites," I am baffled. For is not this just the challenge that Freud is addressing in *The Man Moses and the Monotheistic Religion*? This is why I am stymied by your concluding sentence – that the task "has hardly begun" – unless you mean it to be ironical. For whatever your ultimate judgment concerning the validity of the claims made in *The Man Moses and The Monotheistic Religion*, the study is intended to help "clarify, in a nonreductive way, what unconscious needs are being satisfied at any given time by living within a given religious tradition."

Something has gone wrong; there is a gap in your reasoning. Let me suggest what I think this gap is. Freud's main contribution to our understanding of a religious tradition is to make us acutely aware of how much is unconsciously conveyed and communicated even in "direct communication." It is not just, as you declare, that the "basic modalities" in the continuity of a religious tradition are interpreted by the unconscious as well as by consciousness, but that there are also unconscious traces that mark what is communicated by precept, example, narrative, etc. This deepening of the concept of communication and tradition stands at the very center of Freud's understanding of psychoanalysis. This does not mean that what is directly communicated can be reduced or explained away by an appeal to the unconscious, but rather that we must learn to discern the traces of the unconscious in direct communication. In short, we need to pay attention not only to the "unconscious needs" that are being satisfied in a religious tradition, but also to traces of unconscious processes in the modalities for the continuity of a tradition. Most "traditional" concepts of tradition – even sophisticated hermeneutical concepts – rarely pay attention to this dimension of the handing down of a tradition. But this unconscious aspect of the transmission of a tradition is crucial for understanding why certain narratives, precepts, and examples have such powerful psychological effects on the recipients. Despite your sensitivity and sympathy with Freud, despite the fact that you emphasize that the true axis of the *Moses* book is Freud's reflections on the concept of a religious tradition, you do not do justice to this aspect of Freud's rethinking of what a tradition means, a tradition in which we must understand the subtle interplay of conscious and unconscious memory-traces. Sometimes it seems to me that you slip into thinking that there is a sharp dichotomy between "direct communication" (where this is understood as a *conscious* process) and "unconscious communication" which is presumably based on a discredited theory of the transmission of acquired characters. This is what I have called the "picture" that appears to hold you captive. But this is the very picture that Freud is calling into question. We might even say that he is deconstructing it.

I also want to suggest a hypothesis about why this misleading picture holds you captive – even though you frequently cite the very texts from Freud that can be used to deconstruct it. The clue is to be found in your subtitle: "Judaism Terminable and Interminable." You suggest that Freud's "stand upon the reality of an archaic unconscious inheritance forged out of the historical experience of our ancestors and transmitted 'independently of direct communication' . . . served a 'powerful inner personal need'"(*FM*, 89). Addressing yourself to Freud, you write:

For if a "national character" (those are your words) can indeed be transmitted "independently of direct communication and education by example," then that means that "Jewishness" can be transmitted independently of "Judaism," that the former is interminable even if the latter be terminated. And thus the puzzle that so plagued you about your own Jewish identity would seem to be resolved (and the subtitle of this book incidentally explained). (*FM*, 89–90)

Freud did believe that Jewishness (or more accurately, what Freud took to be the essence of Jewishness) could be transmitted independently of "Judaism." Freud, like many secular Jews, wants to affirm that we can make a sharp distinction between Judaism and Jewishness. But unlike many other secular Jews, Freud does not maintain that it is the customs, narratives, rituals, and ceremonies that are vital for Jewish identity and continuity. This may well be an impossible position to defend, and Freud never squarely faced the seeming paradox of whether (and how) Jewishness can endure without Judaism. But I do not think (as you seem to) that he sought to base his conviction that Jewishness can persist without Judaism on a "discredited Lamarckism." I suggest that the reason that you keep reiterating this accusation is because *you* – as a superb scholar of Jewish history – cannot accept the sharp distinction that Freud draws between Judaism as a religion and Jewishness as a defining character of the Jewish people. Although I am sympathetic with a critique of the way in which Freud draws this distinction, I do not think that it can be dismissed by claiming that Freud thinks that Jewishness is "interminable" because it is biologically transmitted. But this is the basis for your criticism of Freud. In your discussion of the passage from "*Der Fortschritt in der Geistigkeit*" where Freud tells the story of Rabbi Jochanan ben Zakkai, you write:

If there was also a parable here for the new psychoanalytic diaspora, it rested squarely on what Freud regarded as a central Jewish experience, ultimately rooted in the qualities which the Jewish religion had impressed upon the Jews for all time. Needless to say, while granting these historically positive effects of Judaism Freud was not attempting to salvage the old religion for the present or the future. Despite its kernel of historical truth, religion was still illusion. Having forged the character of the Jews, Judaism as a religion had performed its vital task and could now be dispensed with.

It is what you go on to say that I find so telling:

For, incredibly and outrageously, Freud was thoroughly convinced that once the Jewish character was created in ancient times it had remained constant, immutable, its quintessential qualities indelible. "According to trustworthy accounts, they behaved in Hellenistic times as they do today. The Jew was, therefore, already complete even then." Though Freud does not put it into words, the conclusion is inescapable. *The character traits embedded in the Jewish psyche are themselves transmitted phylogenetically and no longer require religion in order to be sustained. On such a final Lamarckian assumption even godless Jews like Freud inevitably inherit and share them.* (*FM*, 52, emphasis added)

I do not know if you fully realize that in a passage like this one, you seem to be accusing Freud of the type of racism that became so popular in the nineteenth century, and was to become the backbone of Nazi anti-Semitism. If there are Jewish "character traits" that are "transmitted phylogenetically and no longer require religion," then there is a biological basis for singling out Jews for extermination regardless of their professed religious convictions. This is why I find the claim that you keep reiterating so disturbing – that Freud believes Jewish acquired character traits are phylogenetically transmitted by biological mechanisms. Furthermore, I do not understand how you can reconcile your claim with Freud's *explicit* claim, which I have already cited.

We found that the man Moses impressed this character on them by giving them a religion which increased their self-esteem so much that they thought themselves superior to all other peoples. Thereafter they survived by keeping themselves apart from others. *Mixtures of blood interfered little with this, since what held them together was an ideal factor, the possession in common of certain intellectual and emotional wealth.* (23:123, emphasis added)

Here Freud explicitly denies the importance of biological transmission and positively asserts the importance of an "ideal factor" in Jewish survival.[6]

You are fascinated with the question of whether Freud thought psychoanalysis was a "Jewish science," even though Freud never even raises this question in *The Man Moses and the Monotheistic Religion*. When you indicate your intentions in the "Prelude for the Listener," you declare that "This book is not an attempt to prove that psychoanalysis is 'Jewish,' though eventually it is concerned to inquire whether Freud thought it to be so, which is a very different matter" (*FM*, xvii). I know how extensively this issue has been discussed in the secondary literature (pro and con), but I have never found it gripping,[7] nor am I convinced it has much importance for understanding the *Moses* study. You tell us that deciding whether psychoanalysis is a Jewish science will depend on the (future) definition of "Jewish" and "science," but this is not the question that you want answered – it is rather what Freud himself *believed*. We do not need to waste much time debating whether Freud thought that there was some intrinsic or essential manner in which psychoanalysis is Jewish. Freud never wavered in his conviction that the psychoanalytic hypotheses that he advanced and defended have universal validity. In this respect he stood squarely in the tradition of the *Aufklärung* – from Kant to Habermas. All his life he vehemently opposed any suggestion that psychoanalysis was *intrinsically* a Jewish science.[8] But there is another line of thought grounded in his *Moses* study which you do not adequately pursue. The basic issue with which Freud is struggling is the distinctive character of the Jewish people and the question of Jewish survival. In this respect, his discussion of *Der Fortschritt in der Geistigkeit* has special importance. Freud explores the consequences of the Mosaic prohibition against making an image of God. You have discussed this theme perceptively in your superb article "The Moses of Freud and the Moses of Schoenberg." Freud directly relates the prohibition against images to the advance in intellectuality and spirituality which increased Jewish self-esteem. Furthermore, Freud claims that the Jews not only "retained their inclination to intellectual interests," it has been the crucial factor in their survival as a people. From the way in which Freud characterizes this "advance in intellectuality," this "progress in spirituality," we can see that he thought of psychoanalysis as fitting within this tradition. Considering the times that Freud was living through during the 1930s, there is a special poignancy to his claim that "[t]he [Jewish] nation's political misfortune taught it to value at its true worth the one possession that remained to it – its literature" (23:115). Furthermore "[t]he pre-eminence given to intellectual labours throughout some two thousand years in the life of the Jewish people has . . . helped to check the brutality and the tendency to violence which are apt to appear where the development of muscular strength is the popular ideal" (23:115). Freud is not just referring to the history of the Jewish people, he is alluding to the events that were taking place at the very time he was writing these words. *In this sense then, in the sense in which Freud thought of himself as carrying on this great Jewish intellectual tradition* – furthering *Der Fortschritt in der Geistigkeit*, he would certainly have endorsed the words of his daughter, Anna, that labeling psychoanalysis as a "Jewish science" can "serve as a title of honour"(*FM*, 100). Without in any way compromising its claim to scientific legitimacy and universality, the discipline of psychoanalysis can proudly identify itself with the advance in intellectuality that was bequeathed to the Jewish people by the great man who "created" the Jews – Moses.

Consequently I am perplexed when you write:

I have tried to understand your *Moses* within its stated framework of the history of religion, of Judaism, and of Jewish identity without reading it as an allegory of psychoanalysis. What I have done, whether well or not, stands by itself. But I carry within me a pent-up feeling, an intuition, that you yourself implied something more, something that you felt deeply but would never dare to say. So I will take the risk of saying it. I think that in your innermost heart you believed that psychoanalysis is itself a further, if not final, metamorphosed extension of Judaism, divested of its illusory religious forms but retaining its essential monotheistic characteristics, at least as you understood and described them. In short, I think you believed that just as you are a godless Jew, psychoanalysis is godless Judaism. But I don't think you intended us to know this. Absurd? Possibly. But *tomer dokh* – perhaps, after all . . .? (*FM*, 99)

I agree with you that this is precisely what Freud *believed* – that psychoanalysis understood as a further stage of development of *Der Fortschritt in der Geistigkeit* is a "metamorphosed extension of Judaism, divested of its illusory religious forms but retaining its essential monotheistic characteristics." But why do you think that Freud did not intend us to know this – that he was concealing his true beliefs? On the contrary, like Edgar Allen Poe's "The Purloined Letter," this is not a concealed message, but one which stands right before us – manifest for all to see who read what Freud actually says in his *Moses* book.

Before concluding there is one more issue that I want to discuss with you. For here I disagree with you most emphatically. Toward the end of your "Monologue," after asking "[i]s Oedipus immortal?" and wondering whether "[l]ike Sisyphus pushing his rock, Oedipus and Laius must contend forever" (*FM*, 95), you write:

Le-didakh. Let it be according to you that religion, the great illusion, has no future. But what is the future of Laius and Oedipus? We read to the end of your *Moses*, and you do not say. But should you tell me that, indeed, they have no hope, I shall simply reply – you may very well be right. But it is on this question of hope or hopelessness, even more than on God or godlessness, that your teaching may be at its most un-Jewish. (*FM*, 95)[9]

We both agree that the commitment to hope, even in the face of utter catastrophe, has been a dominant characteristic of the Jewish tradition. Walter Benjamin beautifully captured this conviction when in the darkest of the dark times, he declared: *Nur um der Hoffnungslosen willen ist uns die Hoffnung gegeben* (It is only for the sake of those without hope that hope is given to us).

The question then is not about the significance of hope in the Jewish tradition, but rather about Freud's understanding of hope and hopelessness. You seem to think that the "eternal return" of the cycle of "patricide, repression, return of the repressed, followed by reenactment of the entire cycle, though disguised under different forms, in a seemingly endless spiral" (*FM*, 95) is clear evidence of Freud's sense of "hopelessness." *Le-didakh.* According to you, this is where Freud's teaching is most "un-Jewish." Let me be frank. I am inclined to say that this misses the main point of *The Man Moses and the Monotheistic Religion*. Freud wrote his

Moses book with a painful awareness of the ominous threat to the very survival of the Jewish people. The fundamental theme of the book concerns the vexed Mosaic legacy that has shaped the character of the Jewish people. Freud emphatically affirms that it is this *Geisitigkeit* (intellectual and spiritual) character that has held the scattered people together. It has enabled the Jewish people to survive, to resist brutality. Insofar as *Der Fortschritt der Geistigkeit* defines the character of the Jewish people, there is the promise that they will continue to survive. Is this not what Freud is telling us in his parable of Rabbi Jochanan ben Zakkai? This is not "hopelessness," and it is certainly not "un-Jewish." In the spirit of the prophetic tradition that Freud so admired, it is an expression of a profound hope. Indeed, if I were asked, while standing on one foot, to say what *The Man Moses and the Monotheistic Religion* is about, I would not hesitate to say it is about hope and the promise of Jewish survival.

Repetition – even the repetition of the cycle of repression and the return of the repressed – is no evidence or sign of "hopelessness." Repetition is intrinsic to the Jewish tradition. Every year at Passover, we repeat the story of the Exodus, and the rabbis tell us that we must tell the story as our *own* story from bondage to freedom; not simply as the story of what happened long ago. This is a far more apt analogy for understanding what Freud is saying than the story of Sisyphus pushing his rock. In Freud's "Haggadah" there is also repetition. In every generation there is the danger of losing our freedom, of falling away from the nobility of our tradition, of succumbing to idolatry and the bondage which our archaic heritage opposes.

Let me conclude by repeating those perceptive words about "the return of the repressed" that *you* have quoted from Lou Andreas-Salomé: "But in this case [the Mosaic tradition] we are presented with examples of the survival of the most triumphant vital elements of the past as the truest possession in the present, despite all the destructive elements and counter-forces they have endured" (*FM*, 78).

I have tried to take seriously your own declaration that *Freud's Moses* is a "prolegomenon," and that your primary purpose has been to open a serious discussion, not to close it. It is in this spirit that I have engaged in "dialogue" with you. There is, and can be, no finality to agonistic but friendly *le-didakh*. It is itself a symbol of the survival and hope of the Jewish tradition.

Appendix

An exchange of letters between Sigmund Freud and
Lou Andreas-Salomé[1]

6.1. 1935
Vienna IX, Berggasse 19

My dear Lou

... What you have heard about my last piece of work I can now explain
in greater detail. It started out from the question as to what has really
created the particular character of the Jew, and came to the conclusion
that the Jew is the creation of the man Moses. Who was this Moses and
what did he bring about? The answer to this question was given in a
kind of historical novel. Moses was not a Jew, but a well-born Egyptian,
a high official, a priest, perhaps a prince of the royal dynasty, and a
zealous supporter of the monotheistic faith, which the Pharaoh Amenhotep IV had made the dominant religion round about 1350 BC. With
the collapse of the new religion and the extinction of the 18th dynasty
after the Pharaoh's death this ambitious and aspiring man had lost all
his hopes and had decided to leave his fatherland and create a new
nation which he proposed to bring up in the imposing religion of his
master. He resorted to the Semitic tribe which had been dwelling in the
land since the Hyksos period, placed himself at their head, led them out
of bondage into freedom, gave them the spiritualized religion of Aten
and as an expression of consecration as well as a means of setting them
apart introduced circumcision, which was a native custom among the
Egyptians and only among them. What the Jews later boasted of their
God Jahve, that he had made them his Chosen People and delivered
them from Egypt, was literally true – of Moses. By this act of choice and
the gift of the new religion he created the Jew.

117

These Jews were as little able to tolerate the exacting faith of the religion of Aten as the Egyptians before them. A non-Jewish scholar, Sellin, has shown that Moses was probably killed a few decades later in a popular uprising and his teachings abandoned. It seems certain that the tribe which returned from Egypt later united with other kindred tribes which dwelt in the land of Midian (between Palestine and the west coast of Arabia) and which had adopted the worship of a volcano god living on Mount Sinai. This primitive god Jahve became the national god of the Jewish people. But the religion of Moses had not been extinguished. A dim memory of it and its founder had remained. Tradition fused the god of Moses with Jahve, ascribed to him the deliverance from Egypt and identified Moses with priests of Jahve from Midian, who had introduced the worship of this latter god into Israel.

In reality Moses had never heard the name of Jahve, and the Jews had never passed through the Red Sea, nor had they been at Sinai. Jahve had to pay dearly for having thus usurped the god of Moses. The older god was always at his back, and in the course of six to eight centuries Jahve had been changed into the likeness of the god of Moses. As a half-extinguished tradition the religion of Moses had finally triumphed. This process is typical of the way a religion is created and was only the repetition of an earlier process. Religions owe their compulsive power to the *return of the repressed*; they are reawakened memories of very ancient, forgotten, highly emotional episodes of human history. I have already said this in *Totem and Taboo*; I express it now in the formula: the strength of religion lies not in its *material*, but in its *historical* truth.

And now you see, Lou, this formula, which holds so great a fascination for me, cannot be publicly expressed in Austria today, without bringing down upon us a state prohibition of analysis on the part of the ruling Catholic authority. And it is only this Catholicism which protects us from the Nazis. And furthermore the historical foundations of the Moses story are not solid enough to serve as a basis for these invaluable conclusions of mine. And so I remain silent. It suffices me that I myself can believe in the solution of the problem. It has pursued me throughout the whole of my life.

Forgive me, and with cordial greetings from your

Freud

[Göttingen, mid-January 1935]

Dear Professor Freud:

That you really answer me yourself, recounting the story in such a long letter written in your own hand – how can I thank you adequately for this! I have been carrying the letter round with me for three days, thinking about it all and longing to write to you about it. But even today this is nothing more than a brief exclamation – and partly one of horror, naturally, that all this material should remain unpublished within the corpus of your work. You are quite right of course; you are the best judge of what is going on in Austria. Only it is such a sorrow for us all. And the most essential ingredients of the story seem so inevitably part and parcel of what you have always thought, already so to speak 'in print' long ago, that it is hard to believe that its publication would seriously affect the situation. And the fact that you enlist in your cause a 'non-Jewish scholar', who already discussed the Moses question from the historical and Christian point of view, is surely in your favour.

In this discussion one point struck me as surprising: namely how the 'Semitic tribe' to which Moses resorted seems thereby to some extent diminished or subordinated compared with the kindred tribes and the Egyptian tribes. This tribe now became the inheritor of the Moses tradition; first corrupted it (as the others had done) and then experienced from time to time the precious gift of the return of the repressed, but retained nevertheless this combination of higher and lower elements?

The insights which you gained into all religions by way of the Jewish problem extend for you, as you mention yourself, right back to *Totem and Taboo*. But what particularly fascinated *me* in your present view of things is a specific characteristic of the 'return of the repressed', namely, the way in which noble and precious elements return despite long intermixture with every conceivable kind of material. It is of course 'historical' and not 'material truths' which secretly exercise real power, but within these past historical periods it was after all intensely real psychical forces whose lofty character remained unobliterated.

Hitherto we have usually understood the term 'return of the repressed' in the context of neurotic processes: all kinds of material which had been wrongly repressed afflicted the neurotic mysteriously with phantoms of the past, because in them he sensed something primevally familiar, which he felt bound to ward off. But in this case we are presented with examples of the survival of the most triumphantly vital elements of the past as the truest possession in the present, despite all the destructive elements and counter-forces they have endured. And as in the case of the original religion of Moses, such positive aspects of the process may have been at work also in other religions, and so there too the repressed was not confined to pathological survivals. Whatever strange things may have gone on in the soul of primitive man, which seem to us in later times from our more enlightened standpoint to be so obviously archaic and distorted, these things nevertheless include elements of psychical power which later receded behind intellectual, emotionally weakening forces . . .

In deep gratitude,

Yours,

Lou

Notes

1 Sigmund Freud, *The Standard Edition of the Complete Psychological Works of Sigmund Freud*, translated under the editorship of James Strachey (London, The Hogarth Press, 1953–74), vol. XIII, p. xv. The letters here are © 1966 and 1972 Sigmund Freud Copyrights Ltd and Ernst Pfeiffer: reproduced by kind permission.

THE EGYPTIAN ORIGIN OF MONOTHEISM AND THE MURDER OF MOSES

1 Sigmund Freud, *The Standard Edition of the Complete Psychological Works of Sigmund Freud*, 24 vols., translated under the editorship of James Strachey (London, The Hogarth Press, 1953–74), vol. XIII, p. xv, emphasis added.

Totem and Taboo was originally published in 1913. This preface dated "Vienna December 1930" was first published (in German) in 1934 (*Gesamelte Werke* vol. XXIV [London: Imago Publishing Co., Ltd., 1948], p. 569.). The German text is as follows:

Keiner der Leser dieses Buches wird sich so leicht in die Gefühlslage des Autors versetzen können, der die heilige Sprache nicht versteht, der väterlichen Religion – wie jeder anderen – völlig entfremdet ist, an nationalistischen Idealen nicht teilnehmen kann und doch die Zugehörigkeit zu seinem Volk nie verleugnet hat, seine Eigenart als jüdisch empfindet und sie nicht anders wünscht. Fragte man ihn: Was ist an dir noch jüdisch, wenn du alle diese Gemeinsamkeiten mit deinen Volksgenossen aufgegeben hast?, so würde er antworten: Noch sehr viel, wahrscheinlich die Hauptsache. Aber dieses Wesentliche könnte er gegenwärtig nicht in klare Worte fassen. Es wird sicherlich später einmal wissenschaftlicher Einsicht zugänglich sein.

Für einen solchen Autor ist es also ein Erlebnis ganz besonderer Art, wenn sein Buch in die hebräische Sprache übertragen und Lesern in die Hand gegeben wird, denen dies historische Idiom eine lebende "Zunge" bedeutet. Ein Buch überdies, das den Ursprung von Religion und Sittlichkeit behandelt, aber keinen jüdischen Standpunkt kennt, keine Einsohränkung zugunsten des Judentums macht. Aber der Autor hofft, sich mit seinen Lesern in der Überzeugung zu treffen, dass die voraussetzungslose Wissenschaft dem Geist des neuen Judentums nicht fremd bleiben kann. Wien, im Dezember 1930.

The Hebrew translation finally appeared in 1939. Freud consistently expressed both his estrangement from all religion – his atheism – and his "feeling of solidarity" with the Jewish people.

Compare Freud's preface with his remarks from an address delivered on his behalf to the Viennese society of B'nai B'rith. The occasion was his seventieth birthday (May 6, 1926).

What bound me to Jewry was (I am ashamed to admit) neither faith nor national pride, for I have always been an unbeliever and was brought up without any religion though not without a respect for what are called the 'ethical' standards of human civilization. Whenever I felt an inclination to national enthusiasm I strove to suppress it as being harmful and wrong, alarmed by the warning examples of the peoples among whom we Jews live. But plenty of other things remained over to make the attraction of Jewry and Jews irresistible – many obscure emotional forces, which were the more powerful the less they could be expressed in words, as well as a clear consciousness of inner identity, the safe privacy of a common mental construction. And beyond this there was a perception that it was to my Jewish nature alone that I owed two characteristics that had become indispensable to me in the difficult course of my life. Because I was a Jew I found myself free from many prejudices which restricted others in the use of their intellect; and as a Jew I was prepared to join the Opposition and to do without agreement with the 'compact majority' [The reference is to Ibsen's *Enemy of the People*.]. (20:273–4)

2 *The Man Moses and the Monotheistic Religion: Three Essays* is the literal translation of the German original, *Der Mann Moses und die monotheistische Religion: Drei Abhandlungen* (Amsterdam: Verlag Albert de Lange, 1939). My reasons for using this literal translation rather than the standard English title, *Moses and Monotheism*, will eventually become clear. To anticipate, the apparently awkward redundancy of the original German title is directly related to the substantive theses that Freud defends. It is the *man* Moses who, according to Freud, "created the Jews." The character of monotheism and its centrality for the Jewish tradition is Freud's central concern. Furthermore, monotheism as a *religion* is to be understood as a stage in the historical development of religions.

Although Freud accepted the proposed English translation, *Moses and Monotheism*, when Katherine Jones (with the help of her husband Ernest Jones) translated the book into English, he strongly objected when the publisher, Leonard Woolf, proposed the shorter title *Moses*. In his letter to Freud dated 15 March, 1939, Woolf wrote: "I understand from Dr. Jones that you do not like the idea of having the title *Moses* and want it to remain *Moses and Monotheism*. From the publishing point of view it is, I am sure, a great mistake to have the long title, for in England many people will be frightened by the word monotheism. Would you, therefore, agree to its appearing under the shorter title?" (*The Letters of Leonard Woolf*, ed. Frederic Spotts [New York: Harcourt, Brace, Jovanovich, 1989], p. 337). Freud rejected Woolf's suggestion. For a further discussion of the title and its translation, see Yosef Hayim Yerushalmi, "Freud on the 'Historical Novel': From the Manuscript Draft (1934) of *Moses and Monotheism*," *International Journal of Psycho-Analysis* 70 (1989), 375, n. 2. I have followed the practice of citing the James Strachey translation from the *Standard Edition (The Standard Edition of the Complete Psychological Works of Sigmund Freud*, translated under the editorship of James Strachey, London: The Hogarth Press, 1953–74), even though Katherine Jones's less literal translation is more felicitous and closer to the spirit of Freud's German prose. In a few significant places, I have cited Jones's translation, and when I do so I clearly indicate the departure. Quotations from the *Standard Edition* of the work are reproduced by arrangement with Mark Patterson & Associates.

3 Salo Baron, the great Jewish social historian (and the teacher of Yerushalmi), wrote one of the first reviews of *The Man Moses and the Monotheistic Religion*. Although Baron's review is respectful and judicious, he nevertheless characterizes the work as "a magnificent castle in the air" (Salo Wittmayer Baron, review of *Moses and Monotheism*, by Sigmund Freud, *American Journal of Sociology* 45 [1939], 477). In the sixty years since the publication of Freud's book, most scholars (Egyptologists, Jewish historians, anthropologists, and ethnologists) agree with Baron's early judgment.

4 See Yosef Hayim Yerushalmi, *Freud's Moses: Judaism Terminable and Interminable* (New Haven: Yale University Press, 1991). Quotations from this work, © Yale University Press, are reproduced by kind permission of the Press. In addition, see Yerushalmi's *HN*; and, "The Moses of Freud and the Moses of Schoenberg: On Words, Idolatry, and Psychoanalysis," *The Psychoanalytic Study of the Child* 47 (1992), 1–20. Jacques Derrida discusses Yerushalmi's *Freud's Moses* in *Mal d'Archive* (Paris: Editions Galilee, 1995). An English translation "Archive Fever: A Freudian Impression" was first published in *Diacritics* 25 (1995), 9–63. It has recently been published by the University of Chicago Press (*Archive Fever: A Freudian Impression*, trans. Eric Prenowitz [University of Chicago Press, 1996]). This text is based on a lecture given on 5 June, 1994 at an international conference entitled "Memory: The Question of Archives" which was held in London. (All page references are to the University of Chicago Press edition.) See also Jan Assmann, *Moses the Egyptian: The Memory of Egypt in Western Monotheism* (Cambridge, Mass.: Harvard University Press, 1997). Assmann's book became available only when I was completing the first draft of this book. His subtle discussion of Freud in the context of his "mnemohistory" enormously enriches our understanding of *The Man Moses and the Monotheistic Religion*.

I should also like to mention the book by Emanuel Rice, *Freud and Moses: The Long Journey Home* (Albany: State University of New York Press, 1990). Although Rice and Yerushalmi were aware that they were both writing about *The Man Moses and the Monotheistic Religion*, and were dealing with the more general question of Freud's Jewish background, neither had available the manuscript of the other when writing their books. Yerushalmi focuses primarily on Freud's "conscious intentionality" whereas Rice freely speculates about Freud's unconscious intentions. I am far more sympathetic to Yerushalmi's approach. Nevertheless both authors argue that Freud had a much more extensive knowledge of the Hebrew language and the Jewish tradition than he frequently acknowledged in his public statements and in his private correspondence. Both authors argue that Jakob Freud's Hebrew dedication in the Freud family Bible – a gift that he gave to his son on the occasion of Sigmund's thirty-fifth birthday – is of central importance for understanding *The Man Moses and the Monotheistic Religion* as well as Freud's Jewish identity.

5 See Paul Ricoeur, *Freud and Philosophy: An Essay in Interpretation* (New Haven: Yale University Press, 1970), especially Book I, chapter 2 "The Conflict of Interpretations."

6 For Freud's own summary (based on his 1934 manuscript draft), see the excerpt from his letter to Lou Andreas-Salomé dated 1 June, 1935 which is reproduced in the Appendix (*Sigmund Freud and Lou Andreas-Salomé: Letters*, ed. Ernst Pfeiffer, trans. William and Elaine Robson-Scott [New York: Harcourt, Brace, Jovanovich, 1972]). There has been some variation in the transliteration of Egyptian names. Freud preferred "Ikhnaton" as the transliteration of the name of the Egyptian pharaoh who introduced monotheism, and Yerushalmi follows Freud in this usage. The more commonly accepted transliteration (used by Strachey) is "Akhenaten."

7 The fragment entitled "Family Romances" originally appeared in Otto Rank's *Der Mythus von der Geburt des Helden: Versuch einer psychologischen Mythendeutung* (Leipzig: F. Deuticke, 1922), without any title or indication that it was written by Freud. It was published under Freud's name in 1931 as "*Der Familienroman der Neurotiker.*" See Strachey's note (9:236) for further publication details. Strachey also indicates Freud's earlier references to "family romances." For a detailed analysis of the exposure myth, see Michael P. Caroll, "'Moses and Monotheism' Revisited," *American Imago* 44 (1987), 15–35.

8 Despite the lack of "objective evidence" to support the hypothesis that Moses was an Egyptian, there has actually been a very old tradition dating back to Greco-Roman paganism in which it was firmly believed that Moses was an Egyptian. For an account of this tradition, see John Gager, *Moses in Greco-Roman Paganism* (Nashville, Tenn.: Abingdon Press, 1972). Gager tells us:

The existence of such traditions about Moses as an Egyptian priest is attested by Manetho and Apion. In Josephus, Pseudo-Manetho identifies Osarsiph, an ancient priest of Heliopolis, with Moses. Josephus attributes a similar statement to Apion: "Moses, as I have heard from the elders (*presbuteroi*) of the Egyptians, was an Heliopolitan . . ." Two facts emerge from these remarks of Manetho and Apion: first, that Moses was known among certain Egyptians as a local priest of Heliopolis and second, that the tradition existed already in the first century BCE . . . (ibid., p. 40)

Several of Freud's other central claims about the Egyptian Moses are anticipated in this tradition. Gager notes that Strabo says that "Moses became disenchanted with the conditions in Egypt and departed for Judea . . . In particular, Moses' motive was dissatisfaction with the Egyptian understanding of the deity, i.e., theological in the proper sense. He faults the Egyptians and the Libyans for likening the deity to animals and the Greeks for fashioning images of the deity in human form. In contrast he proposes his own definition: 'God is the one thing which encompasses us all, including heaven and earth,' to which Strabo adds: 'which we call heaven and earth and the essence (*physis*) of things'" (ibid., pp. 40–41).

See also Jan Assmann's erudite and imaginative study, *ME*. Assmann, a leading Egyptologist, introduces a basic distinction between history and collective cultural memory. His study is primarily a contribution to mnemohistory – the history of the memory and the "construction of Egypt" in the West. Mnemohistory is a branch of history, but "[u]nlike history proper, mnemohistory is concerned not with the past as such, but only with the past as it is remembered . . . The past is not simply 'received' by the present. The present is 'haunted' by the past and the past is modeled, invented, reinvented, and reconstructed by the present" (*ME*, 8–9). Assmann brilliantly demonstrates that throughout Western history there has been a Moses/Egypt discourse in which it has been claimed that Moses was an Egyptian. Although Freud himself was not fully aware of this tradition, Assmann argues that *The Man Moses and the Monotheistic Religion* can be read as a culmination of this tradition. Assmann is concerned with the fate of what he calls the "Mosaic distinction" – the distinction between true and false in "the counter-religion" of monotheism. Assmann argues that Freud "deconstructs" the counter-religion of monotheism which was originally introduced by the historical Egyptian pharaoh Akhenaten and which has been ascribed to Moses – "a figure of memory but not of history" (*ME*, 2).

9 Yerushalmi sharply criticizes this "pivotal" assumption in Freud's argument. I discuss Yerushalmi's objections in my "'Dialogue' with Yerushalmi," pp. 91–7.

10 James Strachey translates the German word "*geistig*" as "spiritual and intellectual." The precise meaning(s) of "*geistig*" and its cognates is extremely important for understanding how *The Man Moses and the Monotheistic Religion* provides an answer to the questions raised in the preface to the Hebrew edition of *Totem and Taboo*. See my discussion on pp. 31–5.

11 "Akhenaten" means "Beneficial for the Aten" or "Aten is satisfied."

12 Freud based his claims about the monotheism of Akhenaten on the pioneering work of James Breasted who was a great admirer of this heretical Egyptian pharaoh, and even calls him "the first individual in human history." Freud quotes this remark (23:21). More recent scholars have seriously questioned whether Akhenaten's religion was a true monotheism. See Theopile James Meek, "Moses as Monolatrist," and John A. Wilson "Was Akhenaton a Monotheist?" Both articles are in Robert J. Christen and Harold E. Hazelton (eds.), *Monotheism and Moses: The Genesis of Judaism* (Lexington, Mass.: D.C. Heath and Co., 1969). See also W.F. Albright, *Archaeology and the Religion of Israel* (New York: Anchor Books, 1969). Emanuel Rice discusses the controversy concerning the religious beliefs of Akhenaten and Moses in *Freud and Moses*, pp. 138–43.

Jan Assmann does think that Freud was correct in characterizing Akhenaten's religion as "revolutionary monotheism." This monotheism claims both universality and exclusivity. Akhenaten's monotheism was a "counter-religion" – counter to the more traditional Egyptian polytheism. But this historical Egyptian monotheism was obliterated shortly after Akhenaten's death. It was not until the re-discovery of Amarna in the nineteenth century – the archaeological dig that captured the imagination of Freud – that there was a full appreciation of the "revolutionary monotheism" that Akhenaten introduced. "King Amenophis IV, who changed his name to Akhenaten of Akhanyati ('Beneficial for the Aten') and ruled Egypt for seventeen years in the middle of the fourteenth century BCE, is the first founder of a monotheistic counter-religion in human history. Freud was correct in stressing this point" (*ME*, 169). But Assmann also claims that Freud misunderstood the amoral naturalism of the Amarna religion. "Nature itself is amoral. Freud was astonishingly blind to this amoral aspect of Amarna religion. Instead, he stressed its strongly ethical character, which he based on an epithet of the king who called himself 'living on truth/justice'" (*ME*, 190).

13 Recent scholars have corrected the dates of Akhenaten's reign, placing it closer to 1360–1340 BCE.

14 Freud is referring to the hymns to Aten which were discovered at Tel el-Amarna. For an English translation of these hymns, see James H. Breasted, *The Dawn of Conscience* (New York: Charles Scribner's Sons, 1933), pp. 281–9. Breasted comments that "[i]n these hymns there is an inspiring universalism not found before, either in the thought of Egypt or in that of any other country" (ibid., p. 289). Breasted also notes a number of striking similarities between the most important of these hymns and the biblical Psalm 104.

Freud never mentions an article (which he read when it was published) by Karl Abraham, "Amenhotep IV: A Psycho-analytical Contribution Towards the Understanding of his Personality and of the Monotheistic Cult of Aton," in *Clinical Papers and Essays on Psycho-Analysis* (London: The Hogarth Press, 1955); first published (in German) *Imago* 1 (1912), 334–60. Many of Freud's claims about Akhenaten are anticipated by Abraham's article, and appear to be based upon them. Abraham emphasizes that Amenhotep IV (Akhenaten) brought about a "spiritual revolution" (*geistige Revolution*) in religion, ethics, philosophy, and art. Abraham points out – as does Freud – that "[i]t must be particularly emphasized that Ikhnaton did not worship the sun as a god, but that he personified in Aton the warmth of the sun as a life-giving power" (ibid., p. 274). He notes that in forbidding all pictorial representation of this god, Akhenaten was a "forerunner of Moses the lawgiver" (ibid., p. 275). Abraham, however, does not suggest that Moses was an Egyptian aristocrat who was a follower of Akhenaten. Furthermore, according to Abraham's interpretation, it was Akhenaten's mother, Queen Tiye, who influenced her son and was the primary instigator of the monotheistic religious reform. "Immediately after the death of Amenhotep III, the widowed queen made it clear how strongly she inclined towards the cult of Aton, and how important it was for her to use her young son as the instrument of her plans for reform" (ibid., p. 269). Although Abraham sees Akhenaten as "a prophet of monotheism" whose teachings contain "essential elements of the Jewish monotheism of the Old Testament," he agrees with the Egyptologist Arthur Weigall "that Ikhnaton's conception of god has more in common with the Christian than with the Mosaic conception" (ibid., p. 275). For a discussion of Freud's parapraxis in omitting any mention of Abraham's study, see Leonard Shengold, "A Parapraxis of Freud's in Relation to Karl Abraham," *American Imago* 29 (1972), 123–59. See also the discussion of this parapraxis (especially the significance of Freud's neglect of "the model of femininity" in Abraham's portrait of Queen Tiye) by Estelle Roith in *The Riddle of Freud: Jewish Influences on his Theory of Female Sexuality* (London: Tavistock Publications, 1987), pp. 170–5. See also Assmann's perceptive analysis of these hymns in *ME*, chapter 6, "Conceiving the One in Ancient Egyptian Traditions."

15 For a very different but perceptive *political* interpretation of these murmurings, see Michael Walzer, *Exodus and Revolution* (New York: Basic Books, 1985), especially chapter 2, "The Murmurings: Slaves in the Wilderness." In Walzer's political interpretation of the Exodus narrative he does not mention Freud. Nevertheless there is some convergence in their interpretations of the "murmurings." Walzer writes: "The Israelite slaves could become free only insofar as they accepted the discipline of freedom, the obligation to live up to a common standard and to take responsibility for their own actions. They did accept a common standard: hence the Sinai covenant . . .; but they also resented the standard and feared the responsibility it entailed" (ibid., p. 53).

16 This "slide" from conjecture to fact is repeated in Part III when Freud claims that Sellin established the fact [*Tatsache*] "that the Jews, who, even by the account in the Bible, were headstrong and unruly towards their lawgiver and leader, rose against him one day, killed him and threw off the religion of the Aten which had been imposed on them, just as the Egyptians had thrown it off earlier" (23:60–61). For a discussion of Sellin's arguments and Freud's appropriation of them, see Robert A. Paul, "Freud, Sellin and the Death of Moses," *The International Journal of Psycho-Analysis* 75 (1994), 825–37.

17 The biblical cadence of this passage is even more apparent in German.

Da erhoben sich aus der Mitte des Volkes in einer nicht mehr abreissenden Reihe Männer, nicht durch ihre Herkunft mit Moses verbunden, aber von der grossen und mächtigen Tradition erfasst, die allmählich im Dunkeln angewachsen war, und diese Männer, die Propheten, waren es, die unermüdlich die alte mosaische Lehre verkündeten, die Gottheit verschmähe Opfer und Zeremoniell, sie fordere nur Glauben und ein Leben in Wahrheit und Gerechtigkeit ("*Maat*"). Die Bemühungen der Propheten hatten dauernden Erfolg; die Lehren, mit denen sie den alten Glauben wiederherstellen, wurden zum bliebenden Inhalt der jüdischen Religion. Es ist Ehre genug für das jüdische Volk, dass es eine solche Tradition erhalten und Männer hervorbringen konnte, die ihr eine Stimme liehen, auch wenn die Anregung dazu von aussen, von einem grossen fremden Mann, gekommen war. (*MM*, 91)

18 Ernest Jones, *The Life and Work of Sigmund Freud*, 3 vols., (New York: Basic Books, 1953–7), vol. III, p.192. For a helpful discussion of the differences and changes between the 1934 manuscript and the revised printed book see Grubich-Simitis, *Back to Freud's Texts: Making Silent Documents Speak* (New Haven: Yale University Press, 1996), pp. 191–203. See also Yerushalmi's *HN*.

19 *The Letters of Sigmund Freud and Arnold Zweig*, ed. Ernst L. Freud, trans. Elaine and William Robson-Scott (New York: Harcourt, Brace and World, Inc., 1970), p. 97.

20 For a discussion of Freud's concern about arousing the hostility of the Catholic Church, and his worry about the anticipated reaction of Pater Schmidt, see *FM*, 27–9.

21 The formula to which Freud is referring is: "the strength of religion lies not in its *material*, but in its *historical* truth." For my discussion of this formula, see pp. 68–74.

22 In 1935 Freud added the following sentence to a text that he originally wrote in 1924 (which has been misleadingly labeled "An Autobiographical Study"): "My deep engrossment in the Bible story (almost as soon as I had learnt the art of reading) had, as I recognized much later, an enduring effect upon the direction of my interest" (20:8). For further information about the title and publication details of "An Autobiographical Study," see James Strachey's editorial note (20:3–5).

Freud was also deeply fascinated with Michelangelo's statue of Moses in the Church of S. Pietro in Vincoli in Rome. He went to see this statue during his first visit to Rome in September, 1901, and stood transfixed before it many times on subsequent visits. In 1914, he published his famous paper "The Moses of Michelangelo" anonymously in *Imago*. It was only in 1924 that he publicly acknowledged writing this article. None of the controversial hypotheses about Moses being an Egyptian or the murder of Moses by the Jews that are explored in *The Man Moses and the Monotheistic Religion* are mentioned in "The Moses of Michelangelo." Ironically, according to the "historical account" that Freud gives in his *Moses* book, the Egyptian Moses never was at Sinai. Nevertheless the way in which Freud describes Michelangelo's Moses bears a resemblance to his own later portrayal of Moses. "In this way [Michelangelo] has added something new and more than human to the figure of Moses; so that the giant frame with its tremendous physical power becomes only a concrete expression of the highest mental achievement that is possible in a man, that of struggling successfully against an inward passion for the sake of a cause to which he has devoted himself" (13:233).

TRADITION, TRAUMA, AND THE RETURN OF THE REPRESSED

1 The following is the German table of contents for Part III, "Moses, Sein Volk, und die Monotheistische Religion":
Erster Teil
Vorbemerkung I
Vorbemerkung II
  A Die historische Voraussetzung
  B Latenzzeit und Tradition
  C Die Analogie
  D Anwendung
  E Schwierigkeiten
Zweiter Teil
Zusammenfassung und Widerholung
  a Das Volk Israel
  b Der grosse Mann
  c Der Fortschritt in der Geistigkeit
  d Der Triebverzicht
  e Der Wahrheitsgehalt der Religion
  f Die Wiederkehr des Verdrängten
  g Die historische Wahrheit
  h Die geschichtliche Entwicklung
For an analysis of the differences of the contents betwen the published book and the 1934 draft see Grubich-Simitis, *Back to Freud's Texts*, pp. 197–9.

2 In a footnote Strachey declares that this paragraph is "untranslatable." Compare his translation with the more felicitous translation of Katherine Jones:

> Man found that he was faced with the acceptance of "spiritual" forces – that is to say, such forces as cannot be apprehended by the senses, particularly not by sight, and yet having undoubted, even extremely strong effects. If we may trust to language, it was the movement of the air that provided the image of spirituality, since the spirit borrows its name from the breath of wind (*animus, spiritus*, Hebrew *ruach* = smoke). The idea of the soul was thus born as the spiritual principle in the individual. (Sigmund Freud, *Moses and Monotheism*, trans. Katherine Jones [London: The Hogarth Press and the Institute of Psychoanalysis, 1939; New York: Knopf, 1939], p. 146)

See also Yerushalmi's discussion of "the perils in translating the intractable *Geistigkeit*" in *FM*, 127, n.43.

3 The Kant passage is from Immanuel Kant, *Critique of Judgment*, trans. Werner S. Pluhar (Indianapolis: Hackett Publishing Co., 1987), pp. 134–5. The passage from Schiller is cited by Assmann, *ME*, 128. In chapter 4 of his book, Assmann traces the subtle influences among Reinhold, Schiller, and Kant in their references to Egypt. He shows that Schiller's Moses (based in part on his reading of Reinhold) "is ethnically Hebrew and culturally Egyptian, initiated in all the mysteries of the Egyptians" (*ME*, 127). Furthermore, Assmann

shows how Schiller anticipates Freud. The decisive discovery for Schiller "was the identification of the god of the philosophers, that is of reason and enlightenment, with the deepest and most sublime secret of the Egyptian mysteries and the demonstration that it was this sublime and abstract God that Moses had come to accept in the course of his Egyptian initiation and that he had dared – at least partly – to reveal this God to his people" (*ME*, 126). Neither Reinhold, Schiller, nor Kant knew what was only rediscovered in the nineteenth century and which Freud knew – that there really was a historical Egyptian pharaoh, Akhenaten, who believed in such an "abstract" deity. For a further discussion of Schiller's essay and its possible influence on Freud, see Ernst Blum, "Über Sigmund Freuds: *Der Mann Moses und die monotheistische Religion*" *Psyche* 10 (1956), 367–90.

4 This passage is cited in Willy Aron, "Notes on Sigmund Freud's Ancestry," *Yivo Annual* 11 (1956), 293.

5 Richard L. Rubenstein, "Freud and Judaism: A Review Article," *The Journal of Religion* 47 (1967), 41.

6 In his letter of 1 January, 1935 to Lou Andreas-Salomé, Freud already emphasizes the connection between his *Moses* study and *Totem and Taboo*.

> As a half-extinguished tradition the religion of Moses had finally triumphed. This process is typical of the way a religion is created and was only the repetition of an earlier process. Religions owe their compulsive power to the *return of the repressed*; they are reawakened memories of very ancient, forgotten, highly emotional episodes in human history. I have already said this in *Totem and Taboo*. (*SFLA*, 205; Appendix, p. 118)

7 See A.L. Kroeber, "*Totem and Taboo* in Retrospect: An Ethnological Psychoanalysis," *American Anthropologist* 22 (1939), 48–55.

8 For a discussion of the possible significance of Freud's neglect of the role of Queen Tiye in bringing about the religious reform that Freud ascribes to Akhenaten, see Roith, *The Riddle of Freud*, pp. 171–5. See also Dorothea Arnold's catalogue of the recent (1996) New York Metropolitan Museum of Art exhibition, *The Royal Women of Amarna: Images of Beauty from Ancient Egypt*.

9 This repetition and "continuation of the primal history" is also central for the origin of Christianity. "It is scarcely a matter of indifference or of chance that the violent killing of another great man became the starting-point of Paul's new religious creation as well" (23:89).

10 In *The Language of Psycho-analysis*, Laplanche and Pontalis give the following succinct definition of "acting out":

> According to Freud, action in which the subject, in the grip of his unconscious wishes and phantasies, relives these in the present with a sensation of immediacy which is heightened by his refusal to recognise their source and their repetitive character. (J. Laplanche and J.-B. Pontalis, *The Language of Psycho-analysis*, trans. D. Nicholson-Smith [New York: W.W. Norton & Co., 1973], p. 4.)

In Freud's 1914 paper, "Remembering, Repeating and Working Through," he describes what he means by acting out in a therapeutic situation: "we may say that the patient does not *remember* anything of what he has forgotten and repressed, but *acts* it out. He reproduces it not as a memory but as an action; he *repeats* it, without, of course, knowing that he is repeating it" (12:150).

One of the standard criticisms of Freud is that he too easily and freely applies psychoanalytic concepts that were developed in the context of dealing with patients in therapeutic situations to more general cultural phenomena. Ironically, and *belatedly*, it is the application and extension of Freudian concepts to the understanding of cultural phenomena, especially to collective memory and forgetting, that is proving so fruitful. This is especially evident in recent attempts to understand the traumatic consequences of the Holocaust, the complex forms of forgetting and remembering that this traumatic event has engendered, and the ways in which the dynamics of latency and the return of the repressed have operated. See, for example, Dominick La Capra, *Representing the Holocaust* (Ithaca: Cornell University Press, 1994); Saul Friedlander, "Trauma, Transference and 'Working Through'," *History and Memory* 4 (1992), 39–55; Cathy Caruth, *Unclaimed Experience: Trauma, Narrative, and History* (Baltimore: The Johns Hopkins University Press, 1996); and Cathy Caruth (ed.), *Trauma: Explorations in Memory* (Baltimore: The Johns Hopkins University Press, 1995).

11 Freud, *Moses and Monotheism*, trans. Katherine Jones, p. 84.
12 Caruth, *Trauma*, pp. 7–8.
13 Freud's brief remarks about "Mohammedan religion" and Eastern religions are casual and extremely superficial. They show his bias in favor of Judaism.

> From my limited information I may perhaps add that the case of the founding of the Mohammedan religion seems to me like an abbreviated repetition of the Jewish one, of which it emerged as an imitation. It appears, indeed, that the Prophet intended originally to accept Judaism completely for himself and his people. The recapture of the single great primal father brought the Arabs an extraordinary exaltation of their self-confidence, which led to great worldly successes but exhausted itself in them. Allah showed himself far more grateful to his chosen people than Yahweh did to his. But the internal development of the new religion soon came to a stop, perhaps because it lacked the depth which had been caused in the Jewish case by the murder of the founder of their religion. The apparently rationalistic religions of the East are in their core ancestor-worship and so come to a halt, too, at an early stage of the reconstruction of the past. (23:92–3)

14 H. Hartmann, E. Kris, and R.M. Loewenstein, *Papers on Psychoanalytic Psychology*, Psychological Issues Monograph, no.14, (New York: International Universities Press, 1964), p. 96.
15 Lucille B. Ritvo, "Darwin as the Source of Freud's neo-Lamarckism," *Journal of the American Psychoanalytic Association* 13 (1969), 512.
16 This excerpt from Freud's letter to Karl Abraham (11 November, 1917) is cited by Ernest Jones (*J III*, 312). One of the best and clearest discussions of Freud's "Lamarckism" (as well as Freud's indebtedness to Darwin) is by Lucille B. Ritvo, *Darwin's Influence on Freud* (New Haven: Yale University Press, 1990). Ritvo argues that Freud's neo-Lamarckism owes more to Darwin than to Lamarck. See chapter 2 of her book, "Darwin, Lamarck,

and Lamarckism"; and her article "Darwin as the Source of Freud's neo-Lamarckism." See also Frank J. Sulloway, *Freud: Biologist of the Mind* (New York: Basic Books, 1979).

17 One must be careful not to misinterpret what Derrida is saying here. It may seem that Derrida is presupposing an (uncritical) distinction between biological processes and "quite complicated" linguistic and cultural processes. But – to use Derrida's own words – he, like Freud, is more "careful." Derrida, the master of deconstructing binary oppositions and rigid bounded dichotomies, is calling into question the rigid dichotomy between the biological and its "other" (whether psychological, social, cultural, or linguistic). Although Freud's explicit references to biology and biological evolution in *The Man Moses and the Monotheistic Religion* are incidental and minimal, his understanding of the meaning and the reference of "biological" is *not* to be identified with the meaning of this expression as it is used today in existing biological natural sciences. Here too there is the danger of anachronism – of reading back into Freud our present understanding of what constitutes a biological explanation. Just as I am arguing that Freud is expanding and enriching our concept of tradition, so I would also argue that Freud is expanding and enriching the concept of the biological. Freud is a "biologist of the mind," although to acknowledge this does *not* entail accepting what Frank J. Sulloway means by this phrase. (See the "Epilogue and Conclusion" of Sulloway, *Freud: Biologist of the Mind*.)

18 In *Darwin's Influence on Freud*, Appendix A (pp. 199–201), Ritvo lists *all* of Freud's references to Darwin in his writings. In *The Man Moses and the Monotheistic Religion*, Freud refers to Darwin when he introduces his discussion of "The Latency Period and Tradition" in order to illustrate how a controversial scientific theory can initially be "met with embittered rejection," and be "violently disputed for decades," only to be accepted as "a great step forward towards truth" after a long delayed period (23:66). This example serves as a transition to Freud's discussion of the psychoanalytic concept of latency. It also suggests a parallel between the initial resistance to, and triumph of, Darwin's theory of evolution, and what Freud anticipates will be the eventual triumph of psychoanalysis after a period of "violent" resistance.

19 It may be objected that, strictly speaking, "weak" Lamarckism is not really Lamarckian at all because it leaves open the issue of how memory-traces are transmitted from one generation to another; it does not make the strong claim that these traces are biologically (genetically) transmitted.

The distinction that Henry Edelheit introduces between biological and cultural Lamarckism is also helpful in understanding what Freud claims. He writes:

We must also take another factor into account in our consideration of Freud's Lamarckism, and that is that *human* evolution does in fact have a Lamarckian component. Though we now know that other species (for example, Japanese macaques) develop rudimentary cultures that in a limited way are transmitted by teaching and learning, or by imitation, the extent to which human experience is fixed in language and is in this form transmitted from one generation to the next is unique and, in recent evolutionary time, has been exponentially facilitated by the invention of writing.

Cultural inheritance is Lamarckian, as Peter Medawar has pointed out . . . Human beings do adapt to their environments by means of transmitting from generation to generation an acquired "record" of the experience of the group . . .

Human inheritance is indeed a dual inheritance: Darwinian via the genes, Lamarckian via language and culture. Just as the Darwinian mechanism is embodied in the genetic substance, DNA, so the Lamarckian mechanism is embodied in language. (Henry Edelheit, "On the Biology of Language: Darwinian/Lamarckian Homology in Human Inheritance (with some thoughts about the Lamarckism of Freud)," in *Psychoanalysis and Language*, ed. Joseph H. Smith, M.D., vol. III of *Psychiatry and the Humanities* [New Haven: Yale University Press, 1978], pp. 64–5.)

We must not forget that Freud wrote before the great revolution in molecular biology when the molecular structure of genes was discovered.

Edelheit also makes the following perceptive remark about Freud:

Medawar observed that the Lamarckian character of cultural transmission may account, in general, for a persistent psychological pressure to ascribe Lamarckian mechanisms (erroneously) to genetic evolution. I am suggesting, more specifically, that the critical role of *language* in cultural transmission (a Lamarckian mechanism dependent upon a capacity achieved through a Darwinian evolutionary process) may have been a factor in Freud's Lamarckism, for Freud's stubborn insistence on the heritability of acquired characteristics in the human species derives a measure of justification from the homology of the two mechanisms and the functional evolutionary relationship that exists between them. (ibid., pp. 68–9)

What Edelheit and Medawar call the "Lamarckian character of cultural transmission" is what I have called "weak Lamarckism." Compare these passages from Edelheit with the passage previously cited from Derrida's *AF*.

20 One should also note another anachronism that creeps into the discussion of Freud's Lamarckism, especially when it is contrasted with Darwinianism. Ritvo makes an important point when she writes:

Today, Darwin's name and Lamarck's are readily identified as representing two opposing theories of evolution. Darwin's is commonly assumed to signify evolution by natural selection and Lamarck's the inheritance of acquired characteristics. But their works were not always interpreted in this fashion. The abstraction of these single items from the many faceted theories presented by Darwin and Lamarck obscures, even falsifies, their differences and similarities. (Ritvo, *Darwin's Influence on Freud*, p. 31.)

Ritvo also points out that Freud himself *never* makes this stark contrast between a theory of "natural selection" and a theory of "the inheritance of acquired characteristics."

21 These words are from Schiller's poem, *"Die Götter Griechenlands."* Strachey gives the following literal translation: "What is to live immortal in song must perish in life" (23:101).

22 Hans-Georg Gadamer, *Truth and Method*, 2nd rev. edn., trans. Joel Weinsheimer and Donald G. Marshall (New York: Continuum, 1994).

23 This is Yerushalmi's "literal translation" of the introduction to the 1934 draft (*FM*, 17). He also provides a transcription of the German original (*FM*, Appendix 1,101–3). See his note about a prior publication of this Introduction by Pier Cesare Bori, (*FM*, 119, n.60). See also Grubich-Simitis, *Back to Freud's Texts*, p. 195.

24 In *The Future of an Illusion* (1927), Freud anticipates this distinction when he makes the following comment about "truths contained in religious doctrines":

> We need not deplore the renunciation of historical truth when we put forward rational grounds for the precepts of civilization. The truths contained in religious doctrines are after all so distorted and systematically disguised that the mass of humanity cannot recognize them as truth. (21:44)

And in the Postscript to "An Autobiographical Study" written in 1935 (after the first draft of the Moses study was completed), Freud writes:

> In *The Future of an Illusion* I expressed an essentially negative valuation of religion. Later, I found a formula which did better justice to it: while granting that its power lies in the truth it contains, I showed that that truth was not a material but a historical truth. (20:72)

25 Ludwig Wittgenstein, "A Lecture on Ethics" (1929), repr. *Ludwig Wittgenstein: Philosophical Occasions, 1912–1951*, eds. James Klagge and Alfred Nordmann (Indianapolis: Hackett Publishing Co., 1993), p. 44, emphasis added.

26 This passage is also further evidence of how foreign Freud's thinking is from "strong Lamarckism." He declares that the "mixture of blood" interfered little with the special character of the Jewish people because "what held them together was an ideal factor, the possession in common of certain intellectual and emotional wealth."

27 Freud here emphasizes the very point that Karl Popper criticizes Freud and psychoanalysis for neglecting. Popper claims that one of the major reasons why he proposed the criterion of falsifiability as a demarcation principle for distinguishing scientific theories from pseudoscientific doctrines is because of his own conviction that our intellect very easily goes astray and that nothing is more easily believed by us than what, without reference to the truth, comes to meet our wishful illusions. There is even a parallel between Popper's critical rationalism where he stresses the pattern of "conjectures and refutations" and Freud's characterization of scientific creativity as the "succession of daringly playful fantasy and relentlessly realistic criticism." (This phrase is cited by Grubich-Simitis from a letter that Freud wrote to Ferenczi in 1915. See Sigmund Freud, *A Phylogenetic Fantasy: Overview of the Transference Neuroses*, ed. Ilse Grubich-Simitis, trans. Axel Hoffer and Peter T. Hoffer [Cambridge, Mass.: Harvard University Press, 1987], p. 83. It is also cited by Yerushalmi, [*FM*, 30].)

28 The question of the interplay of temporal modalities in the Moses study is even more complicated than I have suggested – for there is also the question

of the "future" of Judaism and Jewishness. See Derrida's discussion of this modality in *AF*, 71–81.

29 There is an excellent discussion of the subtle and complex interplay of manifest and latent content in Louise J. Kaplan's unpublished paper "The Interplay of Manifest and Latent Content." She argues that the metaphor of foreground and background is more perspicacious than the traditional surface-depth metaphor for understanding the manifest-latent distinction.

ANTI-SEMITISM, CHRISTIANITY, AND JUDAISM

1 In a thought-provoking reconsideration of *The Dialectic of Enlightenment*, Anson Rabinbach shows how Horkheimer and Adorno appropriated and developed Freud's insights from *Totem and Taboo* and *The Man Moses and the Monotheistic Religion* in their analysis of anti-Semitism. They explore the Freudian thesis that the prohibition against making an image of God "was the specific form of a more generalized renunciation of mimesis." And they argue that "the transgression against the prohibition on mimicry, imitation, and archaism is endemic to fascism's sanctioning of the visual image over the written word, and the more specifically evident anti-Semitic obsession with the physiognomic and corporeal marks of Jewishness." See Anson Rabinbach, "Outwitting the Historical Dynamic: Mimesis and the Construction of Antisemitism in Horkheimer and Adorno's *Dialectic of Enlightenment*," in *Between Apocalypse and Enlightenment: Central European Thought in the Shadow of Catastrophe* (Berkeley: University of California Press, 1997).

2 This is a phrase from Freud's letter to his son, Ernst, written when Freud was waiting for permission to leave Nazi Austria. It is also the title of Peter Gay's final chapter of his biography, *Freud: A Life for Our Time* (New York: W.W. Norton & Co., 1988). See this chapter for the details of Freud's final months in Vienna and his arrival in London. For a discussion of the symbolic significance of England and France for Freud, see Carl E. Schorske, "Freud: The Psychoarchaeology of Civilization," in Jerome Neu (ed.), *The Cambridge Companion to Freud* (Cambridge University Press, 1991), pp. 8–24; and Carl E. Schorske, "Freud's Egyptian Dig," *New York Review of Books*, 27 May, 1993, pp. 35–40.

3 See the exchange of letters between Freud and Jones (1 November and 2 November, 1938) where Freud writes "I cannot accept a delay of the publication in English without resistance" and Jones expresses his irritation about being pressed. *The Complete Correspondence of Sigmund Freud and Ernest Jones*, ed. R. Andrew Paskauskas (Cambridge, Mass.: Harvard University Press, 1993), pp. 764–5.

4 Gay, *Freud: A Life*, p. 633.

5 This passage from a letter to Dr. Magarik (4 July, 1939) is cited by Gay, *Freud: A Life*, p. 633.

6 In his eloquent essay, "The Moses of Freud and the Moses of Schoenberg," Yerushalmi compares Freud's Moses with the Moses in Schoenberg's opera,

Moses and Aaron. Yerushalmi contrasts what he calls Freud's "verbal optimism" with Schoenberg's "verbal pessimism." Freud's thinking is biblical insofar as "the Bible is an affirmation of speech and the potency of the word whereas Schoenberg is Maimonidean insofar as he stresses the failures of verbal expression." In his analysis Yerushalmi remarks:

> Only twice, to my knowledge, does [Freud's] confidence in verbal expression falter, both times in trying to define the nature of his Jewishness (see the address to the B'nai B'rith and the preface to the Hebrew translation of *Totem and Taboo*). *He did not rest, however, until he had found the words.* The result was *Moses and Monotheism.* (*MFMS*, 13, emphasis added)

Here Yerushalmi concisely expresses the thesis that I have been defending in this essay.

7 See the Introduction, "Freud's Jewish Identity and its Interpretation" in Sander L. Gilman, *Freud, Race, and Gender* (Princeton University Press, 1993) for a discussion and listing of this literature.
8 See Peter Gay, *Freud, Jews, and Other Germans: Masters and Victims in Modernist Culture* (New York: Oxford University Press, 1978); *A Godless Jew: Freud, Atheism, and the Making of Psychoanalysis* (New Haven: Yale University Press, 1987); and *Freud: A Life*. For a critique of Gay, see Yerushalmi, *FM*, 115, n.25. In several publications Sander L. Gilman has sharply criticized Gay. For a recent succinct statement of Gilman's critique of Gay, see Sander L. Gilman, "Freud et les concepts de race et de sexe," *Revue Germanique Internationale* 5 (1996), 99–122.
9 See Kwame Anthony Appiah, "Cosmopolitan Patriots," *Critical Inquiry* 23 (1997), 618.
10 In their analyses of *The Man Moses and the Monotheistic Religion*, Yerushalmi and Rice attach great significance to the dedication that Freud's father, Jakob, wrote in Hebrew when he gave the family bible – the bible that Sigmund read as a young child – to his son on the occasion of Freud's thirty-fifth birthday, in 1891. This dedication was written in the form of *melitzah*, a literary form that has its origins in medieval Hebrew literature. In *melitzah*, each line is selected from the Hebrew Bible (or other Hebrew sources), and fitted together in order to express a new meaning. Yerushalmi notes that "Melitzah, in effect, recall Walter Benjamin's desire to someday write a work composed entirely of quotations" (*FM*, 71). The richness and poetic power of *melitzah* arise because both the writer and the reader are thoroughly familiar with the context from which each phrase or line is selected. Yerushalmi analyzes the Hebrew dedication, gives an English translation of it, and identifies its Hebrew sources (*FM*, 71–4;104–5). Rice dedicates two chapters to this inscription: chapter 6, "The Biblical Sources of the Hebrew Dedication"; and chapter 7, "The Latent Content of the Birthday Benediction" (Rice, *Freud and Moses*). The following is Yerushalmi's translation:

Son who is dear to me, Shelomoh. In the seventh in the days of the years of your life the Spirit of the Lord began to move you and spoke within you: Go, read in my Book that I have written and there will burst open for you the wellsprings of understanding, knowledge, and wisdom. Behold, it is the Book of Books, from which sages have excavated and lawmakers learned knowledge and judgement. A vision of the Almighty did you see; you heard and strove to do, and you soared on the wings of the Spirit.

Since then the book has been stored like the fragments of the tablets in an ark with me. For the day on which your years were filled to five and thirty I have put upon it a cover of new skin and have called it: "Spring up, O well, sing ye unto it!" And I have presented it to you as a memorial and as a reminder of love from your father, who loves you with everlasting love.

Jakob Son of R. Shelomoh Freid [*sic*]
In the capital city Vienna 29 Nisan [5]651 6 May [1]891

Yerushalmi claims that "it is this Hebrew text of Jakob's alone that offers even the possibility of reaching a psychological understanding of Freud's involvement with Moses, from the *Moses* of Michelangelo to the culminating *Moses and Monotheism*" (*FM*, 74). Freud's study was an act of "deferred obedience." It represents "a fulfillment of Jakob Freud's mandate" (*FM*, 77). "In writing *Moses and Monotheism* [Freud] belatedly obeys the father and fulfills his mandate by returning to the intensive study of the Bible, but at the same time he maintains his independence from his father through his interpretation" (*FM*, 78). Rice's claims are even more extreme. He writes: "The Bible Jakob presented to his son, and the inscription it contained, becomes the Rosetta Stone whose language we must master before we can decode Freud's own ambivalent and deeply personal message in *Moses and Monotheism* (Rice, *Freud and Moses*, p. 29). Rice also develops an elaborate "psychoanalytic" account of the "latent" content of the dedication.

Jakob's Hebrew dedication is a fascinating document. For readers familiar with the Hebrew sources of the phrases in the dedication, it takes on a great deal of meaning. But I do think we must be careful and even skeptical about its potential significance for understanding *The Man Moses and the Monotheistic Religion*. No one has clearly established that Freud knew enough Hebrew to read the original Hebrew dedication. (Both Yerushalmi and Rice suggest that Freud might have concealed his knowledge of the Hebrew language.) Even though Freud had some Hebrew lessons in his youth, he consistently denied, in his public statements and in his *private* correspondence, that he could read Hebrew. For example, in 1930 when Freud acknowledged a gift of a book by A.A. Roback with a Hebrew dedication, he wrote: "I had such a non-Jewish upbringing that today I am not even able to read your dedication which is evidently in Hebrew characters. In later years I have often regretted this gap in my education." (Cited by Gay in *Freud: A Life*, p. 600.)

In the Bible that Freud received as a gift from his father, there is also an

English translation of the dedication following the Hebrew inscription. One wonders why there would be an English translation if Freud could understand the original Hebrew. It was Freud's son, Ernst, who first discovered this Phillippsohn Bible with its Hebrew dedication and its English translation. On the occasion of the one hundredth anniversary of Sigmund Freud's birthday, Ernst wrote:

In the last year of my father's life, shortly after his library had been reestablished in his new Hampstead house in London, he was working at his desk while I was rummaging through the shelves. By chance, I came across an insignificant looking volume bound in black canvas, which I found to be a Bible (in Hebrew and German with a fair number of illustrations), an edition which had been very popular on the Continent about the middle of the last century. The volume had been put together from remnants of the Book of Kings, Samuel, and the nearly complete five Books of Moses. What immediately aroused my interest was the discovery of several Hebrew inscriptions on the outer pages – incidentally opening from the left and not from the right. My father, noticing my enthusiasm, presented me with the book . . . The next page shows an inscription in Hebrew and this is followed by a translation into English with the first and last lines written in the shaky hand of Jacob Freud himself . . . That the language of the translation should be English is most likely explained by the fact that it was made by one of Jacob's sons from his first marriage, both of whom settled in Manchester.

This passage is cited in Rice's *Freud and Moses*, p. 1. See p. 35 for a photographic reproduction of Jacob's Hebrew dedication, and p. 63 for a reproduction of the English translation.

Rice also includes a reproduction (and English translation) of Freud's letter to the Hebrew translator of *Totem and Taboo* dated 11 December, 1938 in which he reiterates his inability to read Hebrew: "I am very pleased to hear that the Hebrew edition of *Totem and Taboo* is about to appear. Since then I have also received a parcel which I believe are the proofs of the book. (I, unfortunately, cannot read Hebrew.)" In the same letter, Freud also indicates that *Moses and Monotheism* is about to appear in German and English, and he hopes that the book may also be translated into the "holy language." "My next book *Moses and Monotheism* will appear in the spring in English and German. Its translation into the holy language would naturally afford me great pleasure. It is a continuation of the theme of *Totem and Taboo*, the application to history of the Jewish religion. I must ask you to consider that its contents might hurt Jewish sensitivity insofar as there is a reluctance to submit the subject to scientific inquiry" (Rice, *Freud and Moses*, pp. 46–7).

A further reason to be cautiously skeptical about the significance of the Hebrew dedication for understanding and interpreting *The Man Moses and the Monotheistic Religion* is that even if one hypothesized that Freud deliberately concealed his ability to understand the original Hebrew inscription, there is absolutely no evidence to indicate that he would know the Hebrew sources for the individual lines of the inscription.

11 Jan Assmann points out that *"Der Mann Moses"* is a direct translation from the Hebrew Bible. It is unclear whether Freud was fully aware of this when he chose the final title of his book.

"The Man Moses" is a translation of Exodus 11:3. It is the only place in the Pentateuch where Moses is referred to in such a distancing manner, and that phrasing is especially conspicuous because it occurs after the reader has already become totally familiar with the figure of Moses. Even more significant, it is the only verse in the Hebrew Bible that alludes to Moses' important Egyptian position: . . . "and moreover, the Man Moses was exceedingly important in the land of Egypt." (*ME*, 149)

For further discussion of the title that Freud finally chose for his book, see *FM*, 55; and Bluma Goldstein, *Redescribing Moses: Heine, Kafka, Freud, and Schoenberg in a European Wilderness* (Cambridge, Mass.: Harvard University Press, 1992), p. 102.

12 This is Katherine Jones's translation, *Moses and Monotheism*, p. 147.

''DIALOGUE WITH YERUSHALMI''

1 Yerushalmi's *Freud's Moses* consists of four lectures and concludes with a "Monologue with Freud." Yerushalmi acknowledges that this monologue is a "fiction." He adopts this rhetorical strategy because he feels "an inner need to speak to you directly and to have the audience eavesdrop, as it were" (*FM*, 81). I have appropriated a variation of this strategy in order to sharpen my differences with Yerushalmi's interpretation of *The Man Moses and the Monotheistic Religion*. Of course, the Freud that Yerushalmi addresses in his "monologue" was dead, but Yerushalmi is very much alive. My primary intention is not to criticize Yerushalmi, but rather to bring out the full power as well as the challenge presented by Freud's interpretation of Moses, monotheism, and the essential character of the Jewish people.

2 See Derrida, *AF*.

3 See Derrida's discussion of the meanings of "impression" in *AF*, 26–31.

4 Yosef Hayim Yerushalmi, *Zakhor: Jewish History and Jewish Memory*, (New York: Schocken Books, 1989), p. 109.

5 For example, in *MFMS* when you describe how we know the unconscious "obliquely," you cite the very passages from Freud that indicate that the unconscious is never totally cut off from our conscious lives but rather undergoes "transformation or translation into something conscious" (*MFMS*, 10).

6 I agree with Jacques LeRider who argues that Freud, in *The Man Moses and the Monotheistic Religion*, sharply repudiates biological and racial representations of Jewish identity. See Jacques LeRider, "Jewish Identity in *Moses and Monotheism*," *The Psychohistory Review* 25 (1997), 245–54.

7 See Yerushalmi's critique of Peter Gay's claim that Freud's Jewish identity has no relevance to his creation of psychoanalysis (*FM*, 115–6, n.25). See also

Derrida's discussion of Yerushalmi's concern about whether Freud believed that psychoanalysis is a "Jewish science" (*AF*, 37ff.).

8 Freud was especially hostile to any suggestion that psychoanalysis might be thought of as a religion rather than a science. This was a major reason for his break with Jung. In a letter to Ferenczi (8 June, 1913), Freud writes:

> On the matter of Semitism: there are certainly great differences from the Aryan spirit. We can become convinced of that every day. Hence, there will surely be different world views and art here and there. But there should not be a particular Aryan or Jewish science. The results must be identical, and only their presentation may vary . . . If these differences occur in conceptualizing objective relations in science, then something is wrong.

Although Freud is emphatic in his insistence that the results of science "must be identical," he continues this letter by remarking:

> It was our desire not to interfere with their more distant worldview and religion, but we considered ours to be quite favorable for conducting science. You had heard that Jung had declared in America that [psychoanalysis] was not a science but a religion. That would certainly illuminate the whole difference. But there the Jewish spirit regretted not being able to join in.

See *The Correspondence of Sigmund Freud and Sándor Ferenczi*, vol. I, 1908–1914, eds. Eva Brabant, Ernst Falzeder, and Patrizia Giampieri-Deutsch under the supervision of André Haynal, trans. Peter T. Hoffer (Cambridge, Mass.: Harvard University Press, 1993), pp. 490–91.

9 See also Derrida's discussion of this passage, and his reservations about your claims concerning "hope or hopelessness" (*AF*, 73–5).

APPENDIX

1 These excerpts are from an exchange of letters between Sigmund Freud and Lou Andreas-Salomé. *Sigmund Freud and Andreas-Salomé: Letters*, ed. Ernst Pfeiffer (New York: Harcourt, Brace, Jovanovich, 1966), pp. 204–7, reproduced by permission of Harcourt Brace.

Bibliography

WORKS BY SIGMUND FREUD

Unless otherwise indicated, all works by Sigmund Freud are from *The Standard Edition of the Complete Psychological Works of Sigmund Freud*, 24 vols., translated under the editorship of James Strachey, London: The Hogarth Press, 1953–74. Original date of publication and volume number are provided.

(1909) "Family Romances," vol. IX.

(1912–13) *Totem and Taboo*, vol. XIII.

(1914) "The Moses of Michelangelo," vol. XIII.

(1914a) "Remembering, Repeating and Working Through," vol. XII.

(1915) "The Unconscious," vol. XIV.

(1925) "An Autobiographical Study," vol. XX.

(1926) "Address to the Members of the B'nai Brith," vol. XX.

(1927) *The Future of an Illusion*, vol. XXI

(1930) *Civilization and Its Discontents*, vol. XXI.

(1934) Preface to the Hebrew Translation of *Totem and Taboo*, vol. XIII.

(1934a) "Vorrede" zur hebräischen Ausgabe von *Totem und Tabu, Gesamelte Werke*, vol. XXIV, London: Imago Publishing Co., Ltd., 1948.

(1935) "Postscript to an Autobiographical Study," vol. XX.

(1939) *Moses and Monotheism*, trans. James Strachey, vol. XXIII.

Moses and Monotheism, trans. Katherine Jones, London: The Hogarth Press and the Institute of Psychoanalysis, 1939; New York: Knopf, 1939.

Der Mann Moses und die monotheistische Religion: Drei Abhandlungen, Amsterdam: Verlag Albert de Lange, 1939.

A Phylogenetic Fantasy: Overview of the Transference Neuroses, ed. Ilse Grubich-Simitis, trans. Axel Hoffer and Peter T. Hoffer, Cambridge, Mass.: Harvard University Press, 1987.

Sigmund Freud and Lou Andreas-Salomé: Letters, ed. Ernst Pfeiffer, trans. William and Elaine Robson-Scott, New York: Harcourt, Brace, Jovanovich, 1972.

The Correspondence of Sigmund Freud and Sándor Ferenczi, vol. I, 1908–1914, eds. Eva Brabant, Ernst Falzeder, and Patrizia Giampieri-Deutsch under the supervision of André Haynal, trans. Peter T. Hoffer, Cambridge, Mass.: Harvard University Press, 1993.

The Complete Correspondence of Sigmund Freud and Ernest Jones, ed. R. Andrew Paskauskas, Cambridge, Mass.: Harvard University Press, 1993.
The Letters of Sigmund Freud and Arnold Zweig, ed. Ernst L. Freud, trans. Elaine and William Robson-Scott, New York: Harcourt, Brace and World, Inc., 1970.

SECONDARY WORKS

Abraham, Karl, "Amenhotep IV (Ichnaton): Psychoanalytische Beiträge zum Verständnis seiner Persönlichkeit und des monotheistischen Atonkultes," *Imago* 1 (1912), 334–60.

"Amenhotep IV: A Psycho-analytical Contribution Towards the Understanding of His Personality and of the Monotheistic Cult of Aton," in *Clinical Papers and Essays on Psycho-Analysis*, London: The Hogarth Press, 1955.

Albright, W.F., *Archaeology and the Religion of Israel*, New York: Anchor Books, 1969.

Appiah, Kwame Anthony, "Cosmopolitan Patriots," *Critical Inquiry* 23 (1997), 617–39.

Arnold, Dorothea, Catalogue of the New York Metropolitan Museum of Art 1996 exhibition, *The Royal Women of Amarna: Images of Beauty from Ancient Egypt*.

Aron, Willy, "Notes on Sigmund Freud's Ancestry," *Yivo Annual* 11 (1956), 286–95.

Assmann, Jan, *Moses the Egyptian: The Memory of Egypt in Western Monotheism*, Cambridge, Mass.: Harvard University Press, 1997.

Ater, M., "A New Look at 'Moses and Monotheism'," *Israel Journal of Psychiatry and Related Sciences* 20 (1983), 179–91.

Bakan, David, *Sigmund Freud and the Jewish Mystical Tradition*, Princeton: D. Van Nostrand, 1958.

Baron, Salo Wittmayer, review of *Moses and Monotheism*, by Sigmund Freud, *American Journal of Sociology* 45 (1939), 471–7.

Bergmann, Martin, "Moses and the Evolution of Freud's Jewish Identity," *Israel Annals of Psychiatry and Related Disciplines* 14 (1976), 3–26.

Blum, Ernst, "Über Sigmund Freuds: *Der Mann Moses und die monotheistische Religion*," *Psyche* 10 (1956), 367–90.

Blum, Harold P., "Freud and the Figure of Moses: The Moses of Freud," *Journal of the American Psychoanalytic Association* 39 (1991), 513–36.

Bori, Pier Cesari, "Moses, the Great Stranger," in *From Hermeneutics to Ethical Consensus among Cultures*, Atlanta: Scholars Press, 1994.

Breasted, James H., *The Dawn of Conscience*, New York: Charles Scribner's Sons, 1933.

Caroll, Michael P., "*Moses and Monotheism* and the Psychoanalytic Study of Early Christian Mythology," *Journal of Psychohistory* 15 (1988), 295–310.

"'Moses and Monotheism' Revisited," *American Imago* 44 (1987), 15–35.

Caruth, Cathy (ed.), *Trauma: Explorations in Memory*, Baltimore: The Johns Hopkins University Press, 1995.
  Unclaimed Experience: Trauma, Narrative, and History, Baltimore: The Johns Hopkins University Press, 1996.
de Certeau, Michel, "The Fiction of History: The Writing of *Moses and Monotheism*," in *The Writing of History*, trans. Tom Conley, New York: Columbia University Press, 1988.
Christen, Robert J. and Hazelton, Harold E. (eds.), *Monotheism and Moses: The Genesis of Judaism*, Lexington, Mass.: D.C. Heath and Co., 1969.
Derrida, Jacques, *Archive Fever: A Freudian Impression*, trans. Eric Prenowitz, University of Chicago Press, 1996. First published in *Diacritics* 25 (1995), 9–63.
  Mal d'Archive, Paris: Editions Galilee, 1995.
Edelheit, Henry, "On The Biology of Language: Darwinian/Lamarckian Homology in Human Inheritance (with some thoughts about the Lamarckism of Freud)," in *Psychoanalysis and Language*, ed. Joseph H. Smith, M.D., vol. III of *Psychiatry and the Humanities*, New Haven: Yale University Press, 1978.
Freud, Anna, "Inaugural Lecture for the Sigmund Freud Chair at the Hebrew University, Jerusalem," *International Journal of Psycho-Analysis* 59 (1978), 145–8.
Friedlander, Saul, "Trauma, Transference and 'Working Through'," *History and Memory* 4 (1992), 39–55.
Gadamer, Hans-Georg, *Truth and Method*, 2nd rev. edn., trans. Joel Weinsheimer and Donald G. Marshall, New York: Continuum, 1994.
Gager, John, *Moses in Greco-Roman Paganism*, Nashville, Tenn.: Abingdon Press, 1972.
Gay, Peter, *A Godless Jew: Freud, Atheism, and the Making of Psychoanalysis*, New Haven: Yale University Press, 1987.
  Freud: A Life for Our Time, New York: W.W. Norton & Co., 1988.
  Freud, Jews, and Other Germans: Masters and Victims in Modernist Culture, New York: Oxford University Press, 1978.
Gilman, Sander L., *The Case of Sigmund Freud: Medicine and Identity at the Fin de Siècle*, Baltimore: The Johns Hopkins University Press, 1993.
  "Freud et les concepts de race et de sexe," *Revue Germanique Internationale* 5 (1996), 99–122.
  Freud, Race, and Gender, Princeton University Press, 1993.
  Jewish Self-Hatred: Antisemitism and the Hidden Language of the Jews, Baltimore: The Johns Hopkins University Press, 1986.
Goldstein, Bluma, *Reinscribing Moses: Heine, Kafka, Freud, and Schoenberg in a European Wilderness*, Cambridge, Mass.: Harvard University Press, 1992.
Griffiths, J. Gwyn, "The Egyptian Derivation of the Name Moses," *Journal of Near Eastern Studies* 12 (1953), 225–31.
Grubich-Simitis, Ilse, *Back to Freud's Texts: Making Silent Documents Speak*, New Haven: Yale University Press, 1996.

Freuds Moses Studie als Tagtraum: Ein biographischer Essay, in *Die Sigmund-Freud-Vorlesungen*, vol. III, Weinheim: Verlag Internationale Psychoanalyse; rev. edn., Frankfurt am Main: Fischer Verlag, 1994.

(ed.), *A Phylogenetic Fantasy: Overview of the Transference Neuroses*, by Sigmund Freud, trans. Axel Hoffer and Peter T. Hoffer, Cambridge, Mass.: Harvard University Press, 1987.

Handelman, Susan, *The Slayers of Moses*, Albany: State University of New York Press, 1982.

Hartmann, H., Kris, E., and Loewenstein, R.M., *Papers on Psychoanalytic Psychology*, Psychological Issues Monograph, no. 14, New York: International Universities Press, 1964.

Jones, Ernest, *The Life and Work of Sigmund Freud*, 3 vols., New York: Basic Books, 1953–7.

Kant, Immanuel, *Critique of Judgment*, trans. Werner S. Pluhar, Indianapolis: Hackett Publishing Company, 1987.

Kaplan, Louise J., "The Interplay of Manifest and Latent Content," unpublished paper.

Klein, Dennis B., *Jewish Origins of the Psychoanalytic Movement*, New York: Praeger, 1981.

Kroeber, A.L., "*Totem and Taboo* in Retrospect: An Ethnological Psychoanalysis," *American Anthropologist* 22 (1939), 48–55.

LaCapra, Dominick, *Representing the Holocaust*, Ithaca, NY: Cornell University Press, 1994.

Laplanche, J. and Pontalis, J.B., *The Language of Psycho-analysis*, trans. D. Nicholson-Smith, New York: W.W. Norton & Co., 1973.

Le Rider, Jacques, "Jewish Identity in *Moses and Monotheism*," *The Psychohistory Review* 25 (1997), 245–54.

Meek, Theopile James, "Moses as Monolatrist," in *Monotheism and Moses: The Genesis of Judaism*, eds. Robert J. Christen and Harold E. Hazelton, Lexington, Mass.: D.C. Heath & Co., 1969.

Miller, Justin, "Interpretations of Freud's Jewishness, 1924-1974," *Journal of the History of the Behavioral Sciences* 17 (1981), 357–74.

Neu, Jerome (ed.), *The Cambridge Companion to Freud*, Cambridge University Press, 1991.

Ostrow, Mortimer (ed.), *Judaism and Psychoanalysis*, New York: Ktav Publishing House, 1982.

Paul, Robert A., "Freud, Sellin and the Death of Moses," *The International Journal of Psycho-Analysis* 75 (1994), 825–37.

Moses and Civilization: The Meaning Behind Freud's Myth, New Haven: Yale University Press, 1996.

Rabinbach, Anson, "Outwitting the Historical Dynamic: Mimesis and the Construction of Antisemitism in Horkheimer and Adorno's *Dialectic of Enlightenment*," in *Between Apocalypse and Enlightenment: Central European Thought in the Shadow of Catastrophe*, Berkeley: University of California Press, 1997.

Rank, Otto, *Der Mythus von der Geburt des Helden: Versuch einer psychologischen Mythendeutung*, Leipzig: F. Deuticke, 1922.

Rice, Emanuel, *Freud and Moses: The Long Journey Home*, Albany: State University of New York Press, 1990.

Ricoeur, Paul, *Freud and Philosophy: An Essay in Interpretation*, New Haven: Yale University Press, 1970.

Rieff, Philip, *Freud: The Mind of the Moralist*, New York: Viking Press, 1959.

Ritvo, Lucille B., "Darwin as the Source of Freud's neo-Lamarckism," *Journal of the American Psychoanalytic Association* 13 (1969), 499–517.

Darwin's Influence on Freud, New Haven: Yale University Press, 1990.

Robert, Martha, *From Oedipus to Moses: Freud's Jewish Identity*, New York: Anchor Books, 1976.

Robertson, Ritchie, "Freud's Testament: *Moses and Monotheism*," in *Freud in Exile: Psychoanalysis and its Vicissitudes*, eds. Edward Timms and Naomi Segal, New Haven: Yale University Press, 1988.

Roith, Estelle, *The Riddle of Freud: Jewish Influences on his Theory of Female Sexuality*, London: Tavistock Publications, 1987.

Rubenstein, Richard L., "Freud and Judaism: A Review Article," *The Journal of Religion* 47 (1967), 39–44.

Schiller, Friedrich, *Die Sendung Moses*, in *Sämtliche Werke*, vol. IV, Munich: Carl Hanser, 1962.

Schorske, Carl E., "Freud's Egyptian Dig," *The New York Review of Books*, 27 May 1993, pp. 35–40.

"Freud: The Psychoarchaeology of Civilization," in *The Cambridge Companion to Freud*, ed. Jerome Neu, Cambridge University Press, 1991.

Sellin, E., *Mose und Seine Bedeutung für die Israelitisch-jüdische Religionsgeschichte*, Leipzig: A. Deicherlsche Verlagbuchhandlung, 1922.

Shengold, Leonard, "A Parapraxis of Freud's in Relation to Karl Abraham," *American Imago* 29 (1972), 123–59.

Simon, Ernst, "Sigmund Freud, the Jew," *Leo Baeck Institute Yearbook* 2, 270–305.

Smith, Joseph H. (ed.), *Psychoanalysis and Language*, vol. III of *Psychiatry and the Humanities*, New Haven: Yale University Press, 1978.

Stemberger, Brigitte, "'Der Mann Moses' in Freuds Gesamtwerk," *Kairus* 16 (1974), 161–225.

Sulloway, Frank J., *Freud: Biologist of the Mind*, New York: Basic Books, 1979.

Szaluta, Jacques, "Freud's Biblical Ego Ideals," *Psychiatry Review* (1994), 11–46.

Timms, Edward and Segal, Naomi (eds.), *Freud in Exile: Psychoanalysis and its Vicissitudes*, New Haven: Yale University Press, 1988.

Wallace, Edwin, "The Psychodynamic Determinants of *Moses and Monotheism*," *Psychiatry* 40 (1977), 79–87.

Walzer, Michael, *Exodus and Revolution*, New York: Basic Books, 1985.

Wilson, John A., "Was Akhenaton a Monotheist?," in *Monotheism and Moses: The Genesis of Judaism*, eds. Robert J. Christen and Harold E. Hazelton, Lexington, Mass.: D.C. Heath & Co., 1969.

Wittgenstein, Ludwig, "A Lecture on Ethics" (1929), repr. *Ludwig Wittgenstein:*

Philosophical Occasions, 1912–1951, eds. James Klagge and Alfred Nordman, Indianapolis: Hackett Publishing Co., 1993.

Woolf, Leonard, *The Letters of Leonard Woolf*, ed. Frederic Spotts, New York: Harcourt, Brace, Jovanovich, 1989.

Yerushalmi, Yosef Hayim, "Freud on the 'Historical Novel': From the Manuscript Draft (1934) of *Moses and Monotheism*," *International Journal of Psychoanalysis* 70 (1989), 375–95.

Freud's Moses: Judaism Terminable and Interminable, New Haven: Yale University Press, 1991.

"The Moses of Freud and the Moses of Schoenberg: On Words, Idolatry, and Psychoanalysis," *The Psychoanalytic Study of the Child* 47 (1992), 1–20.

Zakhor: Jewish History and Jewish Memory, New York: Schocken Books, 1989.

Index